My Season on the Bench with the Runnin' and Gunnin' Phoenix Suns

SEVEN
SECONDS
OR LESS

Jack McCallum

A Touchstone Book
Published by Simon & Schuster
New York   London   Toronto   Sydney

To all those deserving players and coaches

who never made it this far

TOUCHSTONE
Rockefeller Center
1230 Avenue of the Americas
New York, NY 10020

Copyright © 2006 by Jack McCallum
All rights reserved,
including the right of reproduction
in whole or in part in any form.

TOUCHSTONE and colophon are registered trademarks
of Simon & Schuster, Inc.

Designed by William Ruoto

Manufactured in the United States of America

10   9   8   7   6   5   4   3   2   1

Library of Congress Cataloging-in-Publication Data is available

ISBN-13: 978-0-7432-9811-7
ISBN-10:   0-7432-9811-X

For information regarding special discounts for bulk purchases,
please contact Simon & Schuster Special Sales at 1-800-456-6798
or business@simonandschuster.com.

THE 2005–2006 PHOENIX SUNS

MAIN CHARACTERS

Players

STEVE NASH—#13, point guard; franchise go-to guy in more ways than one; earned second straight MVP award during season; laid-back but as skilled at delivering well-timed insult as he is well-timed assist.

SHAWN MARION—#31, forward; nicknamed Matrix for special-effects playing style; had several big games in playoffs; has longest tenure with team; sometimes feels underappreciated.

RAJA BELL—#19, shooting guard; newcomer to team but instantly part of in-crowd; buddies with Nash from time together in Dallas; has combustible temper but good guy; became postseason folk hero.

BORIS DIAW (DEE-OW)—#3, center-forward; newcomer to team; hails from France; argumentative but upbeat; newcomer to team but change of scenery helped—won league's Most Improved Player award.

AMARE' STOUDEMIRE—#32, center, injured in preseason and played only three games; cast in role of shadowy superstar for most of season; team wasn't always sure he was working hard on rehab, but future fortunes are tied to his comeback.

LEANDRO BARBOSA—#10, combination guard; known to everyone as L.B.; hails from Brazil; one of the quickest players in the league.

TIM THOMAS—#8, forward, picked up on waivers late in season; relentlessly upbeat; hits big shots; doesn't exactly distinguish himself with hustle.

EDDIE HOUSE—#50, guard, newcomer; never stops talking and never

1

stops shooting; key for positive team chemistry, though struggled late in the season.

Coaches

MIKE D'ANTONI (DAN-TOE-NEE)—the head man; Coach of the Year previous season and finished second in 2005–06; has casual style of leadership but will show temper; playing and coaching legend in Italy; also became general manager late in season.

MARC IAVARONI (I-VA-RO-NEE)—D'Antoni's lead assistant; handles defensive strategy; won one NBA title as player; nobody works harder on film study but has a sense of humor.

ALVIN GENTRY—has more NBA coaching experience than anyone on the staff; a pro's pro with special knack for offense; keeps everyone loose with stories.

PHIL WEBER—gets down and dirty with players as clinician; prone to aphorisms; a bachelor whose Peter Pan lifestyle is the subject of gentle derision, as well as envy, among coaches.

DAN D'ANTONI—older brother of Mike by four years; first year on staff; playing legend at Marshall University; had kind of life they write country songs about but has settled down.

TODD QUINTER—lead scout so not around much until end of the season; his written observations are respected by the coaches; good guy whose high school hoops career was chronicled by author years ago for small Pennsylvania newspaper.

Front Office

JERRY COLANGELO—president and CEO and seminal figure in the organization; sold the team but still involved in big decisions; suffered a personal blow when son left franchise.

ROBERT SARVER—second on masthead but now running the show as managing partner; made his money in banking; brash and forward, but trying to learn the game.

BRYAN COLANGELO—son of Jerry; was general manager until he left to run Toronto Raptors in February after dispute with Sarver; widely respected around the league and not just for being Jerry's son.

DAVID GRIFFIN—promoted to veep of basketball operations after Colangelo left; savvy talent scout with photographic memory about prospects; also very funny.

JULIE FIE—head of public relations; been around so long she's comfortable traveling with mostly males; professional enough not to cheer but slyly pounds the table when things go wrong for Suns.

Staff

AARON NELSON—head athletic trainer; Steeler fan who rubbed it in after Super Bowl victory; quick-witted and acerbic enough to be a coach.

NOEL GILLESPIE—team video guru who sits in on every meeting and is like an assistant coach; he may have screwed up a clip during the season, but the author never saw it.

THE BACKSTORY

A few weeks before the 2005–06 NBA training camps began, I called Julie Fie, the Phoenix Suns' ace director of public relations, to propose a story idea for Sports Illustrated. *I would be with the team throughout training camp as an "assistant coach" and would then write a story about my experiences. (I may have even said "quote marks around assistant coach" during our conversation.)*

I was looking to do something different, something from the inside. In my twenty-five years at *SI,* which included two decades of following the NBA, I had covered everything from BASE jumping to the world championship of squash, but had never engaged in participatory journalism, unless you count having Shaquille O'Neal back his 350-pound ass into me to demonstrate how he doesn't commit offensive fouls.

Julie said she'd check with the authorities—general manager Bryan Colangelo and coach Mike D'Antoni—and get back to me.

I homed in on the Suns for a variety of reasons, not the least of which was Fie. I had known her for two decades and considered her one of the best in the business, not to mention someone who might actually think it was an idea that would fly. I automatically crossed out a couple dozen or so other PR directors who would either dismiss it out of hand or worked for a head coach who would rather push a mule cart down Broadway while wearing a thong than open a window into the inner workings of his team.

I also knew Colangelo and his father, Jerry, still the team's CEO and president. I knew D'Antoni and his assistant coaches, though not all that well, from interviewing them for a story I had written about the Suns during the previous season. I knew assistant coach Todd

5

Quinter well—I even wrote a few stories about him three decades ago when he was a high school basketball star in Nazareth, Pennsylvania—but, as the team's chief scout, he was away from the team much of the time. I knew Steve Nash and Shawn Marion, the team's veteran stars, though neither was what I would call a professional confidant. I thought they were good guys who might not mind a notebook-carrying dilettante; obviously, any such project would need the blessing of the team's superstars, tacit or otherwise.

The other reasons were purely pragmatic. First, the Suns were probably going to be good; unless a team is *profoundly* bad, like, say, the expansion New York Mets or the 2005–06 New York Knicks, it is almost always better to write about a winner. Winning teams are happy, happy teams talk, talk makes stories. Further, the Suns were coming off of a positively revolutionary season during which they had become one of the most entertaining shows in sports. D'Antoni, having spent most of his playing and coaching career in Italy, did not subscribe to the prevailing NBA wisdom that a fast-break team cannot succeed, and so he built a team around Nash that ran like hell and tossed up three-point shots like so much wedding confetti. And, though no one suggested that D'Antoni and his staff didn't work hard, they seemed to be serious about the idea of not taking themselves seriously. In short, they seemed like good guys to hang with.

Julie called back forty-eight hours later and said, "Buy a pair of sneakers. You're on the staff." So to speak.

There are certain stories that just work out, that through some weird alchemy present a combination of factors that trigger positive feelings in the reader. The preseason "assistant coach" story in *SI* was one of them. Judging from the letters, e-mails, and personal comments I received, people enjoyed the inside perspective, the lively interplay (especially the insults) among the coaches, the details of how players and coaches work together, what the coaches say about other teams, and the participatory/Walter Mitty aspect of the story, i.e., the outsider-amateur getting the chance to do what the insider-pro does. Along with allowing me total access to practices, meetings, and meals, the coaches let me participate in drills here and there. On the first day, Marion nailed me in the face as I held the ball during a shell drill, and I felt I belonged.

Soon after the story ran in *Sports Illustrated,* I was asked to expand it into a book. I had doubts as to whether it would work. As friendly and open as the coaches had been in early October, when workouts and scrimmages were held far from prying eyes, they were not about to allow me to muck up drills during the regular season. But perhaps they would once again grant me the same unfettered access and that would be the essence of the book. The publisher said, "Give it a try." I called D'Antoni and he said, "Sure." It was almost that simple.

I had written one "season-with" book *(Unfinished Business)* after spending a considerable part of the 1990–91 season with the Boston Celtics. I rode the team bus, collected stories from players such as Larry Bird and Kevin McHale, and just generally spent a lot of time hanging around. It was "inside" but not in any way, shape, or form like this would be. I didn't fly with the team when it went charter. Coach Chris Ford didn't invite me to coaches' meetings. I was not allowed into the locker room when the rest of the media wasn't there. I couldn't attend closed practices. So this would be an entirely different book.

When I showed up a couple of weeks into the regular season to begin my research, D'Antoni took, literally, ten seconds to brief the team on the colossal significance of my presence. "You remember Jack from the preseason," D'Antoni said at the beginning of an off-day practice. "He's going to be with us a lot of the time working on, I don't know, a book or something." That was it.

Rarely was I asked to keep something off-the-record. As the man in charge, D'Antoni would usually be the one to say, with a smile, "I'll kill you if this is in the book," or, more seriously, "Don't put this in." But considering the hours and hours I spent with the team from November to June, the requests were entirely reasonable. They came to trust me (I think) and further believed that (a) transparency is the best course, and (b) we don't say that many controversial things anyway.

The season turned out to be, in a word, memorable. It's the only word I can come up with. Going into the season, the Suns looked weaker on paper than they did last season because two starters, Quentin Richardson and, most significantly, Joe Johnson, had been traded. Their leading scorer, Amare' Stoudemire, went down with an injury in training camp and missed all but three games. Their supposed lone defensive presence, Kurt Thomas, missed the last two months of the regular season and played only a few garbage-time minutes in one playoff game. Their instant offense off the bench, Leandro Barbosa, missed twenty-five games with various injuries. Their fire-and-brimstone guard, Raja Bell, managed to get himself suspended for an elimination game against the Los Angeles Lakers. On it went.

But they always—*always*—seemed to have something in reserve. Just when it appeared that Nash had played himself into a state of utter fatigue, he would summon up some uncommon effort and hit a shot down the stretch. Just when it appeared that Marion was out of sorts and frustrated by having to guard bigger opponents, he would break loose and win a game almost by himself. And the franchise players were by no means the only source of miracles. Consider: During the playoffs, Phoenix got no fewer than three game-saving or game-winning shots from players (Bell, Tim Thomas, and Boris Diaw) who weren't even with the team last season.

More to the point, they did it their way. By returning to the "old" way of playing, they in fact did something very new. By going back, they moved the game forward. By looking to the past, when teams acted instead of reacted, they were revolutionary.

Truth be told, the Suns advanced further than I thought they would. When you're close to a team, you see not only their strengths but also their weaknesses, of which the Suns had many. You see the process at work, how long and difficult it is, how many minidramas have to play out, how many extraordinary moments have to be coaxed out of players, who, like everybody else on this planet, suffer crises of confidence from time to time. Off the court, the players and coaches were pretty ordinary guys; on it, they did some pretty extraordinary things.

The parameters of my access were simple: I went where the coaches did. I attended their meetings, accompanied them to practice, and sat in the coaches sections of the plane and the bus on road trips, usually next to Dan D'Antoni, the older brother Mike had brought aboard as an assistant. But for me, a journalist who for four decades has been on the outside looking in, nose pressed to the glass, it wasn't that simple suddenly becoming an insider.

I never walked through the Suns' training room, verboten to anyone except team personnel (more than once I saw a player's agent chased out of there), without feeling that I didn't belong, even though everyone welcomed me. I set all kinds of rules for myself. I wouldn't accept an employee pass, and, instead, spent a considerable amount of time snaking my way by any means possible into US Airways Center (which, before January 6, was known as America West Arena) for early-morning coaches' meetings. Yes, I ate the food on the team plane (but not too much), drank the bottled water in the coaches office, and plucked grapes from the pregame fruit plate. But I tried not to avail myself of the postgame buffet that sat, appetizingly, on a table in the locker room.

I went to great lengths to prevent my fellow journalists from seeing me step off a bus or get into a locker room before the prescribed press time. I literally dove for cover when NBA-TV filmed practices at which journalists were not supposed to be in attendance. I was able to insinuate myself behind the bench for many games but refused to adopt what Phil Weber, an assistant coach, calls "the State of the Union look" (white shirt, red tie) to help sell the idea to security guards and other arena personnel that I was actually a coach.

During the season, I wrote about the Suns for *Sports Illustrated* only once—a long piece about Steve Nash, in which he came across glowingly but no more so than if I hadn't been with the team. (I hope that's the case anyway.) When it came time to vote for end-of-the-season awards, I thought of recusing myself but finally decided I could vote fairly. I put Nash in third place (behind Detroit's Chauncey Billups and Cleveland's LeBron James) in the voting for MVP and put D'Antoni second behind San Antonio's Gregg Popovich for coach of the year. Nash won anyway. D'Antoni finished second, jokingly making the claim, whenever I was in earshot, that "one vote for Popovich spun the whole process upside down in some weird way," preventing him from winning for the second straight year.

I didn't hang out with the players much when the coaches weren't around. For one thing, it's not like their first thought was, "Man, we really want some fifty-six-year-old interloper dude going clubbing with us." But there is also a precise line of demarcation between players and coaches. You can't sit in on all the coaches meetings, then try to pass yourself off as some sort of special-exempt player. There were many times, however, when I would just sit in the locker room and listen to Eddie House's nonstop rap or chat with Shawn Marion, Kurt Thomas, James Jones, or Pat Burke about nothing at all. They are good people, and I enjoyed our conversations.

I had a good enough relationship with a couple players, Nash and Raja Bell in particular, that I could give them a gentle amount of grief, and they could certainly give it back. On the day the team

photo was taken, the coaches insisted that I get into one just for pos-
terity's sake, and, as I stood there, silently urging the photographer to
hurry up and snap, Nash said, "Okay, be careful. The spy's in the picture." On the one occasion that I did pilfer a chicken finger from that
postgame buffet, Nash caught me. "Jack, I hope you're paying for
that," he said with a couple of other reporters around.

In the interest of full disclosure, I did two things that I wouldn't
normally do as a journalist: I got Nash to autograph a jersey for a
charity auction and Raja Bell to autograph for my sister-in-law. She
thinks he's hot.

Going into the project, I was curious about one thing in particular—how do professional coaches deal with losing? I had coached an
eighth-grade team for several years, and, though I don't consider myself a particularly competitive person, the losses would gnaw at my
insides, keep me up nights, and have me on the phone for hours with
my assistant coach trying to deconstruct what went wrong . . . with a
bunch of thirteen- and fourteen-year-olds. What must it be like when
the stakes are high? A basketball coach makes so many decisions during a game—substitutions, out-of-bounds plays, defensive alterations,
time-outs—that any single one of them can have an impact on the
result.

The answer turns out to be: The losses do indeed take a heavy
toll. Coaches don't sleep well. They beat themselves up. They look
terrible in the morning. They catch colds. They suck on candy. They
drink too much caffeine. They snap at each other. Sometimes they
order onion rings and French fries together. Then they come in the
next day and do it again.

I flew back to Phoenix with the team after it had lost a 140–133
triple-overtime game to the Knicks in New York on January 2.
The referees that night had suffered from a case of Madison Square
Garden–itis. The Knicks shot fifty-four free throws compared to just

sixteen for the Suns. Had Kurt Thomas not been called for a phantom foul with eight seconds left, the Suns would've won in regulation. It could hardly have been a more agonizing loss, especially since it came to an inferior team. Security at the private airstrip in Newark took forever. It was raining. The plane didn't take off until 1:15 a.m. Some players had brought along their families (they do that on a few road trips per year) and babies were wailing. I felt like wailing, too, and couldn't imagine how badly I would've felt had I been the one presiding over this godforsaken evening.

"Five hours of freakin' misery awaits," said D'Antoni as he boarded the plane. Then he and his assistants fired up their portable DVDs and watched the game, over and over and over, consigning themselves to their own personal small-screen hell.

Yet, no Suns coach—no coach I've ever known, in fact—wants to give up the life. The highs are too high. Though I never in any way, shape, or form considered myself a member of the team, I understood that feeling for the first time.

For at least seven months a year, NBA coaches spend as much as eighteen hours a day together. And the goal is to spend more—by advancing to the Western Conference finals, the Suns' coaches were together almost constantly from the second week of September until the first week of June. Part of the reason I was accepted into their fraternity, I theorize, was that I supplied relief, a diversion from the never-ending mission of *figuring it out,* a buffer when they got sick of each other.

They have no secrets. If one assistant dozes off on a plane or in the coaches' office, one of the others will pull out a cell phone and snap an unflattering photo of him. They rag each other endlessly about their packing "systems" on road trips and celebrate wildly when one or the other of them forgets socks or brings two different shoes. They shower and dress in locker rooms where space is at a premium and personal fashion peccadilloes become conversational fodder. Weber, for example, tucks his shirt into his undershorts, "a tip I picked up in *GQ*," he says. "Maybe it works in the magazine," says Dan D'Antoni, "but not in real life."

(AUTHOR'S NOTE: "D'Antoni" alone will refer to Mike D'Antoni.)

One day Weber and Dan told me how much pleasure they get out of watching Alvin Gentry take his morning vitamins because it is so difficult for him. I wanted to see it, so we spent fifteen minutes surreptitiously tailing Gentry around the training room as he juggled the pills in his hand and made the conversational rounds. Finally, he grimaced, put a pill on his tongue, took a long slug of water, and violently tilted his head back to get it down. We burst into laughter.

"Let me guess," he said, "you jackasses have been following me."

Studying a coaching staff would be rich material for an industrial psychologist. A delicate political game is played every day, even on staffs as close-knit as the Suns'. Coaches are by nature intensely competitive, their lives defined by the joy of winning and the agony of that alternative eventuality. But they have to find a way to get along, to consider each other's opinions yet make themselves heard in the eternal battle to gain traction within the organization. "There is an almost subconscious vying for attention," concedes Iavaroni. "You want to feel indispensable, you want your credit. But you have to subjugate that for the good of the team."

There is a distinct separation between the head coach and his assistants. Every day it is the head coach who must deal with the owner, the front office, the media, and the cold arithmetic of wins and losses. To the public, the most important person in the franchise is the star player; within the franchise, the most important person is the head coach. It's not even close. "You slide down two feet on that bench," says Gentry, who was once a head coach, "and you just *feel* the difference in pressure."

A head coach has to act like the boss, even a head coach with the easygoing and casual personality of D'Antoni. It might seem like a small matter, but in seven months with the team I never saw

D'Antoni, who is still in good shape, take a shot at the basket or do anything remotely connected to playing. Never. Before and after practice, I frequently shot around with the other assistants (I finished the season with a humiliating 3-13 H-O-R-S-E record against Iavaroni) and watched as they traded shots with and even got into some one-on-one work with the players. But D'Antoni was always the overseer. "Well, hell, why would I want to embarrass myself in front of guys who are the best players in the world?" he said when I asked him about it. My theory, though, is that he held off because, in some small way, it sets him apart. *This is my gym, my practice, my team.*

The theoretical role of the assistant is to give the head man enough information so that he can make his decisions, find his "comfort level," as Weber puts it. But an assistant has to sense when the head man has enough information and doesn't want to hear anything else. "I want every one of my coaches to say whatever the hell they want to say," says D'Antoni. "I want to hear everything. But if I don't follow what they say, I don't want to hear about it afterward." He rarely did. The Suns coaches move forward.

"Having been a head coach and an assistant," says Gentry, "I've seen it from both sides. It's tempting to just throw out suggestions aimlessly when something goes wrong. 'Hey, let's go trap this pick-and-roll.' But if you trap it and they throw it to somebody else and he hits a three, the assistant is not the one who has to explain it. That's on the head coach. That's why you just have to shut the hell up sometimes."

Countless teams have been ripped apart by assistants who curry favor with the star players or the general manager. "Getting your guy fired by backstabbing him," says Iavaroni, "is the most common way to get a head job." Over an entire season, I never saw one instance of that in Phoenix. That doesn't mean it didn't happen or won't happen, particularly if the team starts to lose. But I didn't see it. There were countless times when I was certain that one or a couple of the assistant coaches weren't in complete accord with D'Antoni's game-plan decision. But they never gave off a whiff of their doubt to the team. "Doug Collins used to have a saying when we were in Detroit," says Gentry. " 'Agree or disagree in the room, but, when the meeting's over, align.' We always align."

It was fascinating to watch the interaction of the coaches with each other and with D'Antoni, and he with them. Weber, for example, is below both Iavaroni (the designated lead assistant) and Gentry (the former head coach) on D'Antoni's pecking order, yet he is the assistant most likely to chat up D'Antoni immediately after a time-out is called. It's just Weber's personality. ("White Noise," Gentry calls him.) Iavaroni was schooled in a more formal process in Miami under Pat Riley. "I would never go right to Pat and say, 'Coach, I think we need to do this.' I would make a case with Stan Van Gundy [Riley's lead assistant]. And if Stan thought it was valid, then he would take it to Pat."

Iavaroni knows that D'Antoni doesn't share his insatiable appetite for video, so he reflexively semi-apologizes for it in advance. "I have a lot of clips here, Mike, so any time you want to stop me . . ." The assistants respect each other's territory. During a plane ride between Toronto and Detroit on April 1, Gentry, watching the replay of a game, catches Phoenix's quicksilver guard Leandro Barbosa jumping around on defense when he should just be guarding his man. He tells Dan D'Antoni about it, so that Dan, who had become more or less Barbosa's personal coach, could go back and discuss it with the player. Iavaroni, the de facto defensive coach, feels free to discuss that aspect of the game with any player. But if he happened to catch, say, a flaw in Boris Diaw's shooting, he would tell Weber about it, and Weber, Diaw's shooting coach, would be the one to bring it up.

If any of the assistants detected what they considered to be a major problem with the offense, they would certainly tell D'Antoni about it first, particularly if it involved Nash. Nash and D'Antoni are like quarterback and offensive coordinator. But D'Antoni respected the relationships—Iavaroni and the big men, Weber and Diaw, Dan and Barbosa—the assistants had with individual players, too. And D'Antoni would often count on Gentry, who has the gift for getting along with everyone, to talk to Marion or encourage one of the reserves who hadn't played much.

Part of my motivation for doing the original *SI* story was to demonstrate that NBA coaches do, in fact, coach. While football coaches are venerated for both their acumen and their organizational skills, and baseball managers are cast as mystics, able to turn around the course of a season simply by calling a pitchout, pro basketball coaches are victims of the worst kind of stereotyping. The average sports fan, even some NBA fans, believe that coaches roll out the balls, players pick them up and start firing, and that pretty much constitutes the essence of what the coach does, until one day he gets fired with a year or two still left on his contract. (Or, in the case of Larry Brown, four years with $40 million left.) To watch D'Antoni and his assistants disprove the flawed conventional thinking was a unique privilege.

Some readers may object to the occasional rough language, but this is what sports sounds like. There are faculty meetings, Boy Scout getaways, and, Lord knows, sportswriter bull sessions at which the language is ten times rougher than at a meeting of the Suns coaches or a locker room conversation among players. And if I had been looking to write about indecorous behavior on the road, I chose the wrong team, certainly the wrong coaching staff. Unless you call ordering both onion rings *and* French fries at Johnny Rocket's perverse—and you might—this was a strictly PG season.

Writing in the first person is an implicit act of narcissism, particularly when you are not the focus of the story. But the "I" voice does slip in once in a while and my only excuse is that it was unavoidable. Over time the book became an intensely personal experience, much more so than anything I've ever worked on. I witnessed more than half of the regular-season games and all except one of the playoff games live. That meant I spent quite a lot of time in "America's Sweatiest City," as Phoenix was declared by a publication called *LiveScience,* although from November to April it felt pretty damn good. I went on a dozen road trips and ate countless meals with the coaches. Night life was at a minimum, but Dan D'Antoni and I would share an adult beverage from time to time and solve most of the world's problems. When I wasn't with the team, I followed the Suns through the NBA-TV package, the Internet, and once, while en route to a New Year's Eve party, on satellite radio.

Around the league, I had to accept the joshing I got about my affiliation. P. J. Carlesimo, the San Antonio Spurs' assistant coach, saw me once and said, "Hey, there's the Suns' houseboy." I had no retort.

Family and friends eventually got a case of Suns stroke, too. Chris Stone, my editor at *SI,* had a lot of general NBA business to talk over with me but our conversations invariably began with Phoenix. "You pick up anything about their offense this week?" Chris might ask. Or, "Did Eddie House say anything funny?" My brother-in-law's wedding took place on the night of Game 7 of the playoff series against the Lakers, and I felt terrible about missing it. But when I reached the bride and groom by telephone to congratulate them, their first words were, "We saw the last part of the game in the bar at the reception. Awesome!" They may have had a glass of champagne or two by then.

Most emotionally invested was my wife, Donna, who in thirty years of marriage had never made a single comment about a player or game. One December morning when I was out in Phoenix, I awakened to find this e-mail message from her: "I think that Diaw's really going to be a player!" That's when I knew this was something different.

THE BACKSTORY

It was a fortuitous bonus that the season turned out infinitely more interesting than I thought it would. The postseason was so long and intriguing that the backbone of the book consists of those final six weeks of the season. And so we begin at the end.

—Jack McCallum
August 2006
Stone Harbor, N.J.

PROLOGUE

Phoenix, June 3, 2006 . . . .
GAME 6, WESTERN CONFERENCE FINALS
DALLAS 102, PHOENIX 93

It wasn't until the end—the very end—that Steve Nash truly failed. Through seventy-nine regular-season games (he missed three with injuries) and three enervating playoff series, twenty games, Nash had not always played superbly, but he had always played nobly, attempting to fulfill the myriad responsibilities he had as the Phoenix Suns' point guard and cocaptain. But now, when it was time for him to respond to a question from coach Mike D'Antoni . . .

Steve? You got anything?

The question hung in the air in a hushed Suns locker room in US Airways Center. Shawn Marion, the Suns' other cocaptain, a reluctant talker even in the best of times, had already offered a couple of the requisite banalities. *It was a great season. It was great playing with all you guys. Let's come back strong.* Platitudes, really, but nobody expected anything else. Platitudes are the lingua franca of sports, and, anyway, this was the time for platitudes. D'Antoni himself and Suns' owner Robert Sarver, two men accustomed to holding a stage, had already addressed the group and nothing they had said would ever find its way to *Bartlett's*.

D'Antoni: "All right, guys, unbelievable job. You guys gave everything you had and you should be proud."

Sarver: "I'm really proud of you guys, given the setbacks we had this year. You guys brought it every night and you won your division, fifty-four games, took it all the way to here. But we're gonna be even better next year, come back hard, and you guys did a great job and thank you very much."

Actually, neither D'Antoni nor Sarver thought for a minute that *everyone had given everything they had*. But the Suns, collectively, achieved much more than anyone thought they would and, over the last eight weeks, had done it so dramatically. The Suns had finished the season with one word attached to them: *resilient*. So the message delivered by coach and owner, really, was the only one that made sense.

Steve? You got anything?

How many times during this eventful season—which included injuries, overtime nightmares, a fracture between ownership and front office, battles with referees, a couple of postseason miracles—had Nash dribbled himself into exhaustion, as he had in the dying moments of this season-ending loss to the Mavericks? How many times had he stood in the Suns' locker room, either before a game or at halftime, urging his teammates to get out early and warm up, preparation being one of the principal reasons for his unlikely rise to the top? How many times had he envisioned his Suns beating the Mavericks (the team that two summers ago had let him walk into free agency and into the eager arms of the Suns), the kind of sublime vengeance only a competitive athlete could understand?

Steve? You got anything?

How many times had Nash conversed with either D'Antoni or one of the Suns' other four assistant coaches about strategy, most of those talks predicated toward tweaking an offense that, over the past two seasons, had revolutionized the NBA, even as it left the franchise one agonizing step from a shot at a championship? How many practice jumpers had he launched, trying always to further refine a sweet stroke that was partly responsible for his rise to preeminence among the NBA's point guards?

Steve? You got anything?

For Nash, the season had been bittersweet, as every season is for players with unquenchable ambition and unrealized championship hopes. More sweet than bitter, to be sure. But frustration, doubt, and failure had been dogged companions from October to June, particularly for one so competitive as Nash. Win a second straight Most Valuable Player award . . . but deal with the doubters who say it should've gone to LeBron James, Kobe Bryant, or Dwyane Wade, players with more spectacular athleticism, as well as the whispers that his skin color (white) had something to do with the honor. Play well . . . but play always in pain, too—a congenitally creaky back, tight hamstrings, sore knees, wobbly ankles. Achieve so much as a team without an injured Amare' Stoudemire, an integral part of last year's team . . . but worry that Stoudemire's return next season will upset the delicate chemistry that had been built with new additions such as free-agent shooting guard Raja Bell and multipositioned Atlanta Hawks castoff Boris Diaw, benign additions to the locker room. Be happy for good pal and former Dallas teammate Dirk Nowitzki, whose outside shooting had helped throttle the Suns, and who was going to represent the West in the Finals . . . but be sad that Nowitzki, with whom he had twice broken bread during this Western Conference playoff, had beaten him to the big stage.

Steve? You got anything?

Since Nash arrived in Phoenix (the team that had originally drafted him in 1996 and for which he had played the first two seasons of his career before being traded to Dallas) in the summer of 2004, appearing at his introductory press conference in a pair of golf shoes (the only hard-soled kicks in his closet), he had become the face of the franchise, a face so popular that assistant coach Alvin Gentry once opened a box addressed to him to find a short note, a basketball, and an instant camera. "Could you please get Steve Nash to sign my ball and take a picture of him doing it?" was the plea.

There is not a face like it in all of American pro sports. Nash more closely resembles street urchin than street baller, hollow eyes, long nose, long, straight hair that he brushes away from his eyes and hooks behind his ears, sometimes in mid-play. Nash reads books, dabbles in lefty politics, has a BOYCOTT VEAL sticker plastered to his SUV, and tosses out a little Zen from time to time. "I don't like to build maps," he told me one day at practice after I had asked him if he has a favorite spot on the floor to shoot from. He's Canadian, too, giving him automatic legitimacy as a peace-loving anticapitalist. And so a certain counterculture ethos had settled in around Nash, and, by extension, the Suns.

But the idea of Nash as a symbol of something—the Indie Point Guard, the First Counterculture MVP—in fact obscures the central truth about him: He is first and foremost a gym rat. He doesn't fit in basketball around reading Karl Marx; he reads a little Marx and shoots a million jump shots. Only such a player could lead the D'Antoni revolution.

In the summers of his teen years, D'Antoni, the son of a celebrated high school coach in West Virginia and the younger brother of an outstanding player who is now on his coaching staff, played six hours a day. That included three hours of solitary ballhandling and shooting drills—the hard part that he loved—before three hours of playing pickup games at night. Lewis D'Antoni never pushed his youngest son or gave him much instruction—that came from older brother Dan—but he did free him from summer jobs so he could play ball. When D'Antoni got to Marshall University, he was the one who rounded up every member of his team in the off-season and bugged them about showing up at three o'clock for pickup ball in the gym.

Twenty years later, that's what Nash was doing at Santa Clara University. He and his buddies would be sitting around at night, chilling, talking sports, music, and women, and, when *SportsCenter* came on, that was the signal for Nash to get off his butt. "I felt uncomfortable being comfortable," says Nash. "I'd call the team manager, get the key to the gym, call some teammates, and go shoot for a couple hours."

The careers of player and coach hardly run parallel. Nash maximized his talents, hardened his body, toughened his mind, and, over the last two seasons, played point guard at a level at which only the pass-first greats of the game—Magic Johnson, Bob Cousy, John Stockton—were mentioned. D'Antoni, also a point guard, played in only 130 NBA games, and 50 more for the St. Louis Spirits of the old ABA, and always rued a certain lack of mental toughness, and a dubious outside touch, that kept him from really making it.

But in another time, perhaps, Nash would've been forced to follow the road less taken on which D'Antoni eventually traveled to basketball greatness. D'Antoni came into a league with only seventeen teams (there are thirty now) and precious few roster spots. He was a bit player for two seasons, went to the ABA briefly before the merger with the NBA, then came back with the San Antonio Spurs and got cut. A vision of his future pro basketball life passed before him—a career of splinters and garbage minutes and running the other team's offense during practices, and that was only if he *did* make it back with a team.

So D'Antoni, about whom there was nothing Italian except his surname, packed up and went to Italy to recharge his basketball batteries. He came back for one more try at the NBA, then abruptly left again, and made this break final. He then spent the next ten years blazing his name across European basketball, the Magic Johnson of Philips Milan, the most famous team in the Italian League. He didn't look or act anything like Nash—he has boyish features and a West Virginia aw-shucks approachable demeanor, none of that mysterious Canadian reticence—but, like Nash, he had that ineffable something known as *style*. Italy loved him. He loved Italy. And most of all he loved to play. His coach, Dan Peterson, coined the phrase *sputare sangue*—spit blood—to describe how he wanted his team to play. D'Antoni spat blood. Nash spits blood.

As much as they like and respect each other, and have interests outside of sports, basketball is the central—really the only—connection between D'Antoni and Nash. And when they came together for the first time in the 2004–05 season, the results were electric. Without Nash, the Suns had averaged 94.2 points during the 2003–04 season; with Nash running D'Antoni's offense, they averaged a league-best 110.4. The Suns had won twenty-nine games in 2003–04; with Nash running D'Antoni's offense, they won sixty-two. It was one of the most dramatic turnarounds in NBA history, engineered by a point guard from a hockey nation and a coach who had spent most of his professional life in a country known for pasta and ass-pinching.

When Stoudemire, who averaged almost twenty-seven points per game last season, went down with a knee injury in training camp last October, the supposition was the Suns could not possibly score at last season's clip. D'Antoni insisted they were going to average 110 points, nay, *needed* to average that to be successful. His stated goal was to win fifty games and make the playoffs. They won fifty-four and had the fourth-best record in the NBA. And they came close to 110, too, leading the league with 108.4 points per game and setting all-time records in three-point shots taken and made.

It wasn't as if D'Antoni had invented anything; rather, he had reimplemented a run-and-gun style that had been popular into the late 1980s. It is astonishing the degree to which the casual sports fan has it wrong about the NBA. As with the perception that coaching is little more than rolling out the balls, the casual fan perceives the NBA as a bunch of listless underachievers running around aimlessly, tossing up bad shots, ignoring the rudiments of dribbling and passing, and treating defense as if it were to be avoided like the chipped beef special at Denny's. In point of fact, quite the opposite was going on—too little running, too much stodgy offense, too many defensive schemes, an overcoached product that had removed much of the spontaneity of the game and put a premium on isolation alignments designed to get one player the ball and turn his four teammates into statues.

That's what D'Antoni wanted to change. And so he became the prophet for the new version of run-and-gun, and Nash was the apostle taking the message to the masses. *We have our best chance of scoring before the 24-second shot clock hits 17.* That means they wanted to get a shot up in seven seconds or less from the time they got the ball.

Steve? You got anything?

A dozen pairs of eyes swiveled toward Nash, who was standing in front of his corner locker. He was shirtless, wearing only a pair of black compression shorts. It looked for a moment like he was going to say something, but then you saw the blink of the eyes, the purse of the lips, and, finally, the quick shake of the head. He was crying, and, if he had a platitude to offer, he couldn't get it out. I looked over at one of the Suns' assistants, Alvin Gentry, who, having seen the pain and sadness in Nash, began tearing up himself. Then Nash walked toward D'Antoni and his teammates gathered around. They put their hands together and then it was time for the same ritual that ended every practice and every game. "SUNS!" Marion said. "ONE-TWO-THREE . . ." and everyone shouted "SUNS!"

Nash slung a towel around his neck and kept on going toward the training room, his home away from home, slapping a few team-mates' hands along the way. He put his towel on a stool and climbed into the icy water, a procedure he follows religiously after every practice and game to reduce the swelling in chronically injured areas, which in Nash's case means a large percentage of his body. He winced slightly as he lowered himself into the tub.

The water temperature was fifty-three degrees. Like always.

CHAPTER ONE

[The Second Season]

Phoenix, April 21 . . . .

"The Suns are built for the regular season. Every series is going to be tough for them because when you live by your offensive three-point shooting, then any off-night you could lose a game."

It is generally believed, though not always elucidated, that NBA teams cannot suddenly change their essence when the playoffs come around. You are, to a large extent, what you have been for the previous eight months. But coaches and players are expected to offer the requisite chestnuts—We have a chance to turn this around. We're starting to peak right about now. It's time to make a fresh start—and broadcasters have to declare the official beginning to the Second Season.

After studying the Phoenix Suns at close range all season, I offer this projection about them:

Odds of beating the Los Angeles Lakers in the first round: 2–1.

Odds of beating either the Los Angeles Clippers or the Denver Nuggets in the second round: 5–2.

Odds of winning the Western Conference, probably by beating either the San Antonio Spurs and Dallas Mavericks, and making the Finals: 6–1.

Odds of winning the championship: 10–1.

Another thing that is generally believed—and *always* elucidated—is that fast-break teams like the Suns cannot go far in the playoffs. Tempo inevitably slows down, and that leaves transition teams playing an unfamiliar style. To the purveyors of that belief, which is a vast majority of NBA pundits, the fact that the Suns advanced all the way to the Western finals last season before losing to the San Antonio Spurs proves only that a fast-break team can't make it to the *Finals*. Had the Suns made the championship round and lost to the Detroit Pistons, the axiom would've presumably changed to: A fast-break team can't *win it all*.

Hearing that premise is one of the few things that will turn Mike D'Antoni's sunny disposition cloudy. (Another is a restaurant waiter mispronouncing *bruschetta* with a soft sound in the middle instead of the hard "K" sound, the way the Italians do it, "who, after all, only invented the damn thing.") The coach does not dispute statistics that indicate, yes, scoring usually does go down in the postseason. Nor does he doubt that competitive intensity, which is associated more with defense than offense, goes up significantly, also. But he doesn't see slow-down ball as inevitable. "Coaches hear it, start to believe it, then do it," says D'Antoni, "and it becomes a self-fulfilling prophecy. My point is, it doesn't *have* to be that way. It's not written in stone."

There is, to be sure, an extra buzz about this opening round, given the historical weight of the opponent. Though the Lakers finished in seventh place in the Western Conference, thereby drawing the second-place Suns, they had finished strongly, one of their final victories a 109–89 win over Phoenix on April 16 in Los Angeles. The Suns believe that the Lakers' transition defense is close to nonexistent and will provide an open highway for the Nash-led fast break, so this was the matchup they wanted. D'Antoni couldn't precisely orchestrate it—not in an eighty-two-game season—but the coach had benched Nash and Raja Bell for that late-season game, all but assuring a Laker win that would help them beat out the Sacramento Kings, who were in eighth place.

At the same time, the Suns assume that the Lakers, despite having lost three of four regular-season games to Phoenix and seven in a row before that victory on April 16, also wanted to play them. As hard as the Suns are to defend, there is the general impression that, perhaps, they will let you outscore them—that is more likely to happen in the fox-trot pace of the postseason—and, even if they don't, they won't beat you up physically. Since Kurt Thomas, the Suns' only interior player with a physical presence, went out with a stress fracture in his foot on February 22, the Suns had struggled to an 18-11 record and given up an average of 107.6 points per game, near the bottom in the NBA. Phoenix's further aversion to contact could be demonstrated by the fact that it set an NBA record for both fewest free throws made (14.5) and attempted (18.0). The Suns were deadly accurate from the line but didn't get there much.

Todd Quinter, the Suns' lead scout, feeds this perception in the fifty-page loose-leaf notebook he has prepared for the coaches before each playoff series. (He is already at work on one for the Los Angeles Clippers and Denver Nuggets, one of which Phoenix will be playing should it move on.) The book contains all relevant Lakers statistics, individual tendencies of the players, and even a pie-chart breakdown of the Lakers' offense. (They run "ISO's," which stand for isolations, 30 percent of the time, "side p/r," pick-and-rolls on one side of the court or the other, 22 percent of the time, etc.) To make sure the message gets across, Quinter writes:

> *While watching their last broadcast & postgame shows it was amazing to me how absolutely they dismissed us. They talked about getting home court advantage in the next round already like it was a done deal. For whatever reason their team and staff do not respect us at all!*

Phoenix has in fact become rather the popular upset pick among the scores of seers who lay out their playoff grids in newspapers and cyberspace. Ex–point guard Mark Jackson of ABC, former NBA coach Bill Fitch (picking for NBA.com), and David Dupree, *USA Today*'s respected NBA writer, all pick the Lakers. So does ESPN's Greg Anthony, a particular irritant for the Suns; during a memorable brawl with the New York Knicks several years ago, Anthony came off the bench in street clothes to attack Phoenix point guard Kevin Johnson from behind. "He's a Republican," Alvin Gentry says in dismissing Anthony.

A greater source of irritation is TNT commentator Charles Barkley, whose shadow looms over the franchise. (Insert weight joke here.) Barkley was the star of the 1992–93 team that made it to the Finals and lost in six games to Michael Jordan and the Chicago Bulls. He still lives in Phoenix but harbors some resentment toward the Suns, who traded him to Houston two seasons after that near-championship run. Barkley goes out of his way to praise Nash— "Man, I would've loved to have played with a point guard like Nash"—and even wrote a short essay for *Time* when the magazine picked Nash as one of its "100 Most Influential People." (You think essay, you think Charles Barkley.) But Barkley doesn't buy into the D'Antoni up-tempo style.

"The Suns are built for the regular season," says Barkley. "Every series is going to be tough for them because when you live by your offensive three-point shooting, then any off-night you could lose a game. I think the Suns are always going to struggle just because they don't rebound and they don't play good defense. The game always comes down to rebounding and defense. Your flaws don't show until you play a real good team. I think the Suns are too small to win it all."

The presence of Kobe Bryant adds to the buzz. With the possible exception of hockey, where a hot goalie can win a series himself, in no other sport does one superstar player make such a difference as basketball. Great players rarely win an entire series themselves, but they can win one or two individual games, and the Suns are hardly a mortal lock to begin with. The longer the series goes, the more Bryant can exert his considerable will upon it, especially considering that he averaged 42.5 points against Phoenix in four games during the regular season.

D'Antoni has his history with Bryant, too. Kobe grew up in Italy where his father, former NBA player Joe "Jellybean" Bryant, was enjoying an expatriate career. The star of Italian basketball at that time was none other than D'Antoni, the dashing Milan guard, who wore number 8. Lacking American role models, young Kobe wore 8 in honor of D'Antoni. Before most Suns-Laker games, Bryant stops by the Phoenix bench, and he and D'Antoni exchange a few pleasant-ries in Italian, which both speak fluently. (Bryant, though, has peti-tioned the league to allow him to change his number to 24 in the following season. It's no slight to D'Antoni, but, rather, Bryant's hom-age to what he considers his 24/7 work ethic.)

Raja Bell had his history with Bryant, too. Bell first gained a small measure of fame in the NBA when, as a member of the Philadelphia 76ers, he helped limit Bryant to 7-of-22 shooting in Game 1 of the 2001 NBA Finals. The Sixers won that game in L.A., 107–101, though the Lakers swept the next four to win the title. Early in the season, Bryant, reacting to what he considered Bell's overaggressiveness, el-bowed Bell in the mouth and shoved him, drawing a technical foul. Later in the season, on April 7, with two weeks remaining in this regu-lar season, Bryant had come to US Airways Arena and scored fifty-one against the Suns, the majority of them with Bell as his defender.

The game actually presented a template for how to conquer the Lakers—Bryant got his share, but his teammates never got involved, and the Suns won 107–96—but that gave Bell meager consolation. After saying all the right things to the press, Bell stood in front of his locker, doing well to contain the fury he felt inside. "Way to go, Rah-Rah," he said aloud. "You held him to fitty." (He deliberately used the street pronunciation of "fifty.") Eddie House and Brian Grant, two of the Suns always willing to lift a teammate up, were standing by.

"Rah-Rah, it was like B.G. said about that guy the night that Jordan went off on his ass," said House. "What was his name, B.G.?"

"Keith Atkins," said Grant, naming a former journeyman guard.

"Yeah," says House. "Keith Atkins says, 'Michael got sixty-nine on me, but he earned every one of 'em.'"

Plus, when Bryant was asked about the sometimes contentious scrums between him and Bell, Bryant scrunched up his face, as only Bryant can do, and said, with requisite contempt, "Raja Bell? I got bigger fish to fry than Raja Bell."

I asked Bell for his reaction. "I know exactly what he's doing," says Bell. "He's saying, 'How dare you mention his name in the same sentence as mine?' I understand that. That's how he thinks."

Bryant, meanwhile, has utterly dominated the preplayoff planning of the coaching staff, which is meeting, as is its custom, in the central office on the fourth floor of US Airways Center. A day earlier, the discussion had even turned physical when Dan D'Antoni suggested, half-kiddingly, that he could guard Bryant, or at least keep him off the baseline.

"You could guard Kobe?" Marc Iavaroni asked.

"Yep," said Dan.

"Well, what do you do if Kobe does . . . *this!*" said Iavaroni, lunging his six-foot-eight-inch, 240-pound body forward, inadvertently knocking D'Antoni off his feet and into a wall, as the other coaches collapsed in laughter.

As the defensive guru, Iavaroni is tasked with coming up with a plan. Plus, the Lakers are "his team." The assistants (with the exception of Dan, who is in his first year) divvy up the opponents during the year for careful scrutiny, and the Lakers belong to Iavaroni, meaning that he has already watched them on tape for countless hours. His intelligence will then be combined with Todd Quinter's more detailed scouting report.

It is, however, difficult to out-detail Iavaroni. His father was for many years the supervisor at Kennedy Airport, a man with an organizational mind who made sure the runways were kept clean, and the son has that kind of mind, too. He had a seven-year NBA career as a cerebral, overachieving forward and cut his coaching teeth on Pat Riley's uber-prepared staff in Miami. Phrases such as "Indiana's 42 Fist is our quick curl pinch" tumble easily out of his mouth. "I think even Marc would agree that, left to his own devices, he would spend more time in the room than any of us," says Gentry.

Like players, coaches have tendencies. Gentry tends to conjure up remedies and theories from his rich past, having been a head coach of three teams and an assistant under men like Larry Brown, Kevin Loughery, and Doug Collins. Weber is a relentlessly upbeat clinician and an unshakeable positive thinker who has read over four hundred books with titles like *Power vs. Force: The Hidden Determinants of Human Behavior* and written poems with lines like "So don't wallow in doubt or be crippled by fear/Take positive action and watch both disappear." He never has a bad day. Dan D'Antoni, Mike's older brother who joined the staff this season, coached high school ball in Myrtle Beach, South Carolina, for thirty years. Dan's default strategic position is: *Never mind all the X's and O's, let's just play harder than they do.* Iavaroni calls Dan, affectionately, "The Old Ball Coach."

D'Antoni's coaching instincts are closer to Dan's than to Iavaroni's. Early in the season D'Antoni had a dream in which he had to prepare an academic paper about the season. "But then I found out Marc had already finished his," says D'Antoni, "and I got all worried because I knew mine wouldn't be nearly as good." During a coaches meeting in December, D'Antoni said: "We need to play this lineup— Nash, Bell, House, Marion, and Diaw. Against the Clippers it was real nice; against New York it was real nice. We gotta have people who can make shots."

"But, Mike," said Iavaroni, "that lineup was only out there for a few minutes together."

"But if you watch the game," said D'Antoni, "you just get a better *feel* about it."

It was a constant dialectic between the head coach and his lead assistant: Iavaroni relies on tape and stats, D'Antoni on feel and flow. Art versus science. Quite often, after he has grouped his players into a certain offensive alignment, D'Antoni will say, "All right, from here, we just play basketball."

At the same time, D'Antoni has been around long enough to know that "just playing basketball" or "just playing harder" than the other team isn't enough. And so he relies heavily on Iavaroni's stats and ability to construct a defensive game plan. In preparing for the Lakers, Iavaroni wants to play more traditionally, less like an NBA team, and keep one defender on Bryant so he will be likely to take a lot of shots and freeze out his teammates.

"So the philosophy we use on Carmelo Anthony, Ray Allen, LeBron James, Kobe Bryant is, 'The more involved the superstar, the less involved his teammates,'" says Iavaroni. (When the coaches talk specific strategy about a player or team, they almost always bring in examples from other players and other teams.) "I know it's not real comfortable for us if Kobe is feeling it. But for every shot he makes, the other guys are saying, 'Oh, shit, Kobe's doing it all again.'"

D'Antoni sees some logic to that, but it makes him nervous. "I don't know why sometimes we just don't trap Kobe on pick-and-rolls," D'Antoni says. "Why give him a chance to really get off? Let's say we're going down the stretch and we're two points up. And now you can't turn Kobe off."

Iavaroni: "You can't turn Kobe off down the stretch anyway."

D'Antoni: "Yeah, but what I'm saying is that we might be up ten going down the stretch instead of two if we *didn't* let him get off. You lay back and let him score, which I understand at some level, but why not make him hit hard shots? I've never seen him get everyone involved whether you trap him or not."

Iavaroni: "I saw it on tape this year. A few times. He gets everyone involved and they create a team concept that has blossomed. If his teammates get the ball from him, they play with *his* balls." Iavaroni is so lost in thought that he doesn't even see the joke.

D'Antoni shrugs. He still has forty-eight hours to make the decision. During the endless hours of discussion about Bryant, it comes up often that he can score fifty points and the Suns could still win, as was the case in that April game. This drives Dan D'Antoni to distraction. As a former high school coach, he can't get his mind around the idea that an opponent, no matter how talented, can scorch you with fifty and everyone treats it as normal. "I don't think we should ever just say, 'Kobe can get fifty and we'll be all right,'" says Dan. "We should just say, 'We're gonna play our ass off on him, make him work and get on his ass.'"

Also worrisome are the inevitable defensive switches that will occur; good defenders like Bell and Shawn Marion have a hard enough time stopping Bryant without him running wild against the other Suns.

"I think it's death—*death!*—having Tim Thomas on Kobe," says Gentry. All agree except for Dan.

"We shouldn't be afraid of that," he says. "I expect Tim Thomas to play good defense. He's an NBA player."

"Could you reiterate that?" says Iavaroni with mock seriousness. "You *expect* Tim Thomas to play good defense? You are a trusting soul."

One thing everyone agrees with—it's not a good idea to show a bunch of video snippets of Bryant getting beneficial calls from the officials. "I don't want to mess with Raja's head, and I don't want to mess with Shawn's head," concludes Iavaroni.

The coaches are used to two sets of tapes anyway. They have a "coaches' tape," which contains lots of game footage and lots of mistakes made by the Suns, and a "players' tape," a heavily edited version that is shown at practice and almost never includes egregious errors by players. D'Antoni believes that embarrassment is a poor coaching tool. It is the job of video coordinator Noel Gillespie and his assistant, Jason March, to keep the tapes separate.

One other minor—but irritating—concern is Amare' Stoudemire. Back in October, before the season began, the Suns' superstar-in-the-making had gone down with what was first presumed to be a minor injury to his left knee but subsequently required surgery. Throughout the season, Stoudemire's physical condition had been the Subplot from Hell. He was supposed to come back in late February, but he didn't come back until late March. He was lackadaisical in his rehabilitation even as the Suns tried to sell the idea that he was diligent. By the time his left knee was pronounced fit for duty, his right knee had started to hurt. He came back anyway and played one promising game, one mediocre game, and one disastrous game before the Suns decided to deactivate him again. Then he got arthroscopic surgery on his right knee.

The knee injuries were one thing. But even when he was with the team, he wasn't quite *of* the team. For example, he had left at halftime of the team's April 17 game against the New Orleans Hornets, Fan Appreciation Night, which included a mandatory postgame flesh-press to thank the ticket buyers. (Similar blowoffs by Allen Iverson and Chris Webber in Philadelphia and Zach Randolph in Portland had produced headlines; Stoudemire got away with it.) D'Antoni had thought of telling Stoudemire to stay home during the postseason, or, at least, not having him travel with the team, but decided against it. None of Stoudemire's teammates would've jumped up to protest that move. Now, with the playoffs here, he wasn't always showing up when he should and wasn't always there even when he was there, concentration and intensity being two of Stoudemire's problems.

D'Antoni and assistant general manager David Griffin had thought that they were on the same page with Stoudemire regarding his plans for rehabilitation. They had all decided that Stoudemire would work diligently with the Suns' athletic trainers and try out the knee in the summer with the United States team that would meet for camp in Las Vegas in July, then travel to the Far East for an Olympic qualifier. Stoudemire seemed in accord with the plan, but then told reporters, "I don't think I can play for Team U.S.A. this summer."

And so the Subplot from Hell continues.

CHAPTER TWO

[The Second Season]

April 23 . . . .
GAME 1 OF LAKERS SERIES

"But it's the playoffs now, so, shit, I got to get something ready."

Eddie House stares at the big white greaseboard in the locker room on which Iavaroni has filled almost every inch with tips, reminders, slogans, and stratagems. One hour before tip-off, he is still writing. I ask House if this is the best board he's ever seen.

"Well, no disrespect because this is a good board," says Eddie, gesturing toward Iavaroni, "but, being completely honest, Stan Van Gundy had one hot board." House was with the Miami Heat when Van Gundy was Pat Riley's top assistant. (Riley later resigned as coach and elevated Van Gundy to replace him, only to take back the job, in December 2005, in a sort of reverse palace coup.)

Iavaroni, who had been a Heat assistant with Van Gundy under Riley from 1999 to 2002, agrees with House. He considers Van Gundy to be a board god, the Einstein and Picasso of marker. "Stan had a lot more to work with," says Iavaroni. "He had two boards, really, the top one-third of both filled with offense, the second third with defense, and the bottom third with general stuff." (Now that Van Gundy is gone, Riley has been known to erase and straighten characters that are slightly uneven.) "Someday," Iavaroni jokes, "I hope to give as good a board as Stan." The most important tip Iavaroni has written for this game is his instruction for low-post defense. *Active.*

Leveraged. Unpredictable. "I hope we're not too unpredictable," says Dan D'Antoni, looking at the board, "or we'll unpredict ourselves right out of this thing."

Mike D'Antoni, meanwhile, is in the players' lounge challenging the old-school-style video game. Against all logic, the fifty-five-year-old D'Antoni has the high score on the machine. Mike "Cowboy" Elliott, the Suns' assistant athletic trainer who is thirty years D'Antoni's junior, claims that his higher score was removed by a machine malfunction. "I think Mike pulled the plug," Cowboy says. (When pressed, D'Antoni will concede that Cowboy's score was higher but denies responsibility for its erasure.) D'Antoni says he picked up his video-game chops when he came to Italy. "I was alone in a strange land, and I had absolutely nothing to do except play video games," says D'Antoni. "And this machine is a lot like the one I played in Italy."

Phil Weber theorizes that the players feel relaxed that the head coach can often be found playing video games hours before a game. "It gives them a kind of ease," says Weber, who pays much more attention to the psychological game than any of the other coaches. (In fact, more than any person I've ever known.) "They see the head guy doing it and think, 'Maybe this game isn't all that important. It relaxes them.'"

Forty-three minutes before game time, two minutes after the press evacuated the locker room, the team breaks into two meetings. Iavaroni takes the centers and forwards (the "bigs"), and Weber, Gentry, and Dan D'Antoni talk to the guards and swingmen (the "wings"). D'Antoni remains in his office to fret alone and chew over what he's going to say to the entire group before he sends them onto the floor. Mostly, though, he just chews on popcorn.

The bigs meeting is invariably well organized, given the nature of centers and power forwards (stable and disciplined) and the purposeful bent of Iavaroni's mind. He and D'Antoni arrived together in Phoenix as assistant coaches, but it was always understood that D'Antoni was a little higher, first among equals, the likely next in the line of succession. With eight years as a head coach in Italy (where Iavaroni even played under him for five weeks) and one lockout-shortened season as the head man in Denver, D'Antoni had a track record.

In the off-season, Iavaroni had been a finalist for the head coaching position in Portland that the Trail Blazers eventually gave to Nate McMillan. He is generally considered head coaching timber. But he never acts, as far as I can see, like he's in competition with D'Antoni. Any tension that exists between them relates purely to their stylistic differences, not to Iavaroni's thought that he should be in charge. D'Antoni and Iavaroni (which sounds like a Milanese puppet show) have a bond, in fact, that none of the other coaches share. Both played in the NBA and both won championships, D'Antoni several times as a player and coach in Italy, Iavaroni with the Philadelphia 76ers in 1983. Both have been there at the highest levels of basketball, and that experience simply can't be taught.

Iavaroni plans each pregame bigs meeting down to the second, his minions sometimes moving from the video screen in the players' lounge to the big board in the locker room to another section of the locker room where various individual tips written on orange paper are taped to the wall. The whole thing comes off like a small military operation.

The wings meeting, by contrast, is a study in chaos, given the nature of guards and small forwards (squirrelly, hyperactive, independent). Weber does well to hold the players' attention at all. While Boris Diaw and Kurt Thomas stare stoically at Iavaroni's board and answer his snap-quiz questions, Nash, Bell, and House never stop moving. Bell grabs a cup of coffee. House leaves to use the restroom. Nash jiggles and jerks his body endlessly, wrapping a Thera-Band around his ankles and stutter-stepping across the floor, putting his hands on his hips and twisting his torso, lost in his own personal physiological voodoo. And the coaches can never be sure if Leandro Barbosa, the Brazilian-born speed demon who is being heavily counted on in the postseason, is comprehending anything. The high-

light of the wings meetings comes at the end when they gather together, and, after Weber says, "One-two-three," they all holler
"WANGS!" stretching out the word for several seconds so it becomes
"WAAAAAA-NGS." Quentin Richardson, a swingman who was
traded to the New York Knicks in the off-season, started that tradi-
tion the previous season.

Exactly how much players get out of the board sessions and
scouting reports varies, of course, from player to player. D'Antoni
claims that, when he was an assistant, he would occasionally write, "If
you get this far, come see me" as the fourth or fifth tip on a report.
And no one ever came. Most of the players shrug and say there is too
much detail, and even the coaches admit some of the board is what
they call a CYA (Cover Your Ass) defense mechanism. Surprisingly,
though, no player whom I asked about it says that it's unnecessary.

Shawn Marion is a swing attendee, sometimes going with the
bigs, sometimes with the wings. The joke is that he usually picks the
wrong meeting, listening in on Iavaroni when he's playing small forward, chilling with the wings when his assignment is to guard the
opposition's power forward. Marion is at the wings meeting on this
night even though he will be defending primarily against Lamar
Odom, a power forward. But Odom can also play on the perimeter,
and, in all likelihood, Marion will also have to guard Bryant for sub-
stantial minutes before the series is over. It is a tribute to Marion's
versatility that, on most nights, he *needs* both perimeter and interior
intelligence, though how much he absorbs is a mystery. "Shawn, you
have to work Odom at both ends," says Weber. "He'll get flustered if
you do that."

D'Antoni's pregame speech is straightforward and strategic,
none of those this-is-the-first-step-on-a-long-journey proclama-
tions. He doesn't subscribe much to them. "On Bryant side pick-
and-rolls, we're going to trap them, okay?" says D'Antoni. The coaches
have been talking about little else for the last forty-eight hours, and
no doubt dreaming about how to defense Bryant while they toss and

turn at night, but this is the first time the directive has really been formalized for the players. "Also, don't go for pump fakes [a maneuver used with particular dexterity by Bryant]," says D'Antoni. "In the low post, do your work early and gold when you need to." ("Gold" is the Suns' term for fronting an offensive player, thus discouraging a pass from even being thrown.) D'Antoni's instructions have all been sketched out, sometimes in great detail in the individual meetings, but it is important for the whole team to hear them together. Now there's a plan; now there's a team strategy.

One thing I'm waiting for is the return of Eddie House's pregame dance, which will take place right after the introduction of the starting lineup, the exclamation point on the Suns' ritual of linking arms and rocking from side to side. "I been holding back in the last half of the season," says House. "Didn't want it to get stale. But it's the playoffs now, so, shit, I got to get something ready."

D'Antoni sends the team out, the crowd goes crazy, the lights darken as the Suns' starting lineup—Steve Nash and Raja Bell at guard, Boris Diaw at center, Shawn Marion and Tim Thomas at forward—is announced, the Suns link arms . . . and House finishes by squirming around on his belly, doing the Worm. Game time.

The NBA has become a league of elaborate fraternization, every game beginning with expressions of affection for the opponent, usually in the form of "shugs," those man-hugs that begin with a hand clasp and end with a chest bump or a real squeeze. With trades, free agency, myriad roster moves that have players changing jerseys at a dizzying rate, plus an AAU and elite-summer-camp system that throws players together at an early age, it is hard for a player not to have had some kind of connection with his opponent. And most feel compelled to demonstrate, tactilely, that brotherhood.

There is no such love shown between Kobe Bryant and Raja Bell, however. They arrive at the scorer's table together and walk onto the court without so much as a side glance at each other. This is *the* subplot to watch throughout the series. Bryant does not care much for Bell and certainly does not like the idea that Bell would be considered in any way, shape, or form a "Kobe stopper"; Bell, for his part, despises what he considers to be Bryant's arrogance and perfunctory dismissal of him as an athlete.

The Suns' get-it-and-go offense operates the way it should in the first quarter, putting up thirty-nine points. The problem is, the Lakers get twenty-nine themselves. Bryant is being trapped and doubled and chased out of his spots, but he makes the right pass out of trouble most of the time, and, when he gets space, releases his deadly accurate jump shot. There had been some internal debate that Marion should cover Bryant for stretches, if only to give the Laker superstar a different look, but D'Antoni has decided that Bell will have the primary responsibility. The coach has Raja ready to start the second period, in fact, but, when he notices that Bryant is getting a rest, he orders Bell back to the bench in favor of Barbosa. When Bryant returns, so does Bell.

The Lakers are playing well, and Phil Jackson is playing mind games. After two straight L.A. turnovers, the Laker coach asks referee Bernie Fryer to inspect the ball. He rolls it around in his hands a few times, then tosses it back. "Okay, Bernie," he says.

Around the league, there is a kind of benign resentment of Jackson, who has won nine championships as a coach. The media endlessly debates whether Jackson is just lucky (having had Michael Jordan for six titles in Chicago and both Shaquille O'Neal and Kobe for the other three in L.A.) or good, or some combination of the two, and even Jackson's peer group can't decide. Jackson's reliance on Zen teachings; his carefully cultivated intellectualism; his sly manipulation of the press; his romantic relationship with Jeannie Buss, the daughter of the Lakers' owner Jerry Buss; and, yes, his success and reported $9-million-per-year contract, all make him a logical target, not to mention, at six feet eight inches, an easily located one. Jackson seems determined to be looked on not as a coach, but, rather, as some sort of cosmic seer who uses basketball to communicate higher messages. In a gentle spoof of Jackson, D'Antoni had told the all-employees meeting the day before that he was reading *Zen for Dummies.*

Almost as if he's inviting further criticism, Jackson has taken to coaching from a large, high-backed chair, ergonomically suited to his aching back, hips, and God knows what else. (A former player who got by with guile and a willingness to swing an elbow or two, he appears to be a hundred years old when he gets up and starts walking. And in mid-ambulation, he suggests a skyscraper about to crash slowly to earth.) The chair puts Jackson literally above the crowd, which is where his peer group figures he sees himself anyway. Everyone refers to the chair, obviously, as the Throne. D'Antoni could have the health problems of Toulouse-Lautrec and would never sit in an ergonomic throne.

But the Suns' coaches respect Jackson's coaching chops. Several times over the last couple of days, a stark graphic has appeared on the television: Jackson is 14-0 in first-round series. "He's had great players," says D'Antoni, "but you don't win nine rings and do that well in the playoffs unless you know how to coach." Jackson always selects a ring to wear during the playoffs—this year it's the 2000 version, the first he won with the Lakers.

The Suns lead by 58–50 at halftime, but the atmosphere is tense. Nash, in particular, is being throttled on the perimeter by double-teaming. Kwame Brown is not much of a defender in the eyes of the Suns, but he's a big, agile body, and, when he comes out to help Smush Parker or whoever is guarding Nash, he is effective. The Suns can't get into their offense, and the game is tied 75–75 after three periods. Bryant isn't really killing the Suns, but Bell's offense is worse and Bryant has him in foul trouble with five. The fans try to help out as the inevitable "KO-BE SUCKS" erupts. You could pretty much go into any NBA arena outside of Los Angeles during the season and hear the same cheer.

But Tim Thomas bails out the Suns. At practice the day before, I watched him effortlessly put up three-pointers as Iavaroni tried to distract him. Thomas would get a pass, and Iavaroni would wave a hand in his face or fake a shot toward his nether regions, but Thomas would just smile and launch another, insouciance in a six-foot-ten-inch package. During games, Thomas has begun a ritual by which he waves his own hand directly in front of his face after he makes a jump shot, an indication that nothing can bother him. "I wish he'd take that hand and shove it up his ass," Alvin Gentry said, almost wistfully, after watching it on film a few dozen times. The gesture doesn't quite rise to the level of taunting. But it smacks of taunting. Of all the Suns, though, Thomas appears to be the most impervious to playoff pressure, which is good and bad. He is what Weber calls "a low-flame guy," coasting along at a certain speed, unable or unwilling to shift into a higher gear, but, on the other hand, maintaining almost an eerie calm.

In the end, Nash, playing a mediocre game by his standards, makes the big play. With 1:07 remaining and the Suns leading 98–95, Diaw rebounds a Bell miss and swings it to Nash in the right corner. As D'Antoni screams for his quarterback to bring it back out and kill some clock, Nash lets fly with a three-pointer that goes in, all but sewing up the win. D'Antoni looks skyward, grabs his heart and says, "Oh, shit."

After the game, Nash is told that D'Antoni wanted him to pull it out and get a new clock. "I couldn't hear him," says the point guard, who occasionally likes to good-naturedly stick it to his coach, "but I wasn't going to listen to him anyway."

Thomas, though, is unquestionably the player of the game. He finishes with twenty-two points, including four of five conversions on three-point shots, and also grabs fifteen defensive rebounds, one more than Odom. Bryant also has twenty-two points, his second lowest total since a game on December 23, and is castigated for his passivity; Thomas never seems to be anything *but* passive, yet, in this game, was the determining factor.

Thomas also gets props in the locker room for having raised a lump on Bryant's temple late in the game when the Laker star drove to the basket. Bell had been stopped by a pick, and, as Thomas and Diaw converged to help, Bryant got raked across the face. No call. Immediately after the game, Bryant stalked off the court, glaring at the officials, and later, in the locker room, Bryant showed reporters the lump. Thomas was then asked about it with the assumption that he would deny it. Protocol calls for a guilty party to deny everything, particularly during the playoffs. *He's crazy. I never touched him. If I did, it was incidental contact.* But Thomas just chuckles and says, "I definitely got away with fouling him."

D'Antoni's postgame speech is short. "We didn't play real well," says the coach. "We'll play better next time. Keep it on an even keel. We need fifteen more of these." (Sixteen postseason wins earns you a championship.) There is more a feeling of relief than triumph—the Suns now have a taste of how closely matched the teams might be, and everyone is vaguely wondering why they were not able to dominate a Game 1 at home, normally the surest of victories for a superior team.

"Well, that wasn't real easy, was it?" says Gentry, back in the coaches' office.

"I'm trying to remember the last time it *was* easy," says Iavaroni.

"Back in training camp?" I say.

D'Antoni shakes his head. "If you remember," he says, "it wasn't easy then either."

FULL TIME-OUT

October 7, 2005
TRAINING CAMP, TUCSON

Amare' Goes Down

Alvin Gentry is standing outside the Westin Hotel, waiting for his rental car to arrive from valet, when a distracted Suns' owner Robert Sarver comes wheeling around the circle, practically running over Gentry.

"That's okay, Robert," says Gentry with a smile. "Hit me. I always wanted to own an NBA team."

Sarver gets out of the car, looks at Gentry, and says, "Not today you don't."

Word has just come down that Amare' Stoudemire's left knee, which has kept him out of the last two days of drills, is much worse than anyone had originally thought, bad enough to require an operation. What it did to the Suns' plans for winning a championship was one thing. But it also opened up a schism between Sarver, who had just given Stoudemire a five-year $73-million contract extension, and the Suns' medical and training staffs, as well as between Stoudemire and the team. No one "blamed" him, of course, for having an injured knee. But there was the feeling that part of it was his fault, that the player had let it go too far.

In early August, Stoudemire had complained to Suns' athletic trainer Aaron Nelson about knee pain. But the club had trouble getting the notoriously unreliable Stoudemire to have it checked out. He canceled several appointments for MRI scans, and both Nelson and team orthopedist Thomas Carter, a highly respected surgeon, assumed the knee couldn't have been a major concern for the player. Athletes have aches and pains all the time and have a pretty good

46

sense about which ones are serious. Sarver didn't even know that Stoudemire had been having knee pain.

Stoudemire finally had an MRI scan in mid-September, two weeks before camp began, and it revealed a small lesion in the knee.

The new deal that Stoudemire received had been a fait accompli since his breakout season in 2004–05. Rarely had one player elevated his game so dramatically, from 13.5 points per game as a rookie, to 20.6 the following season, to 26.0 with Nash dishing him the ball during the 2004–05 season. And he had done it so spectacularly, his rim-rattling dunks, sometimes from a standing, two-legged start, having become *SportsCenter* staples. Brian Grant, now with the Suns, said that the Los Angeles Lakers, for whom he played last season, called Stoudemire the Mad Hatter for his audacious, almost crazed eruptions of athleticism. Whether or not Stoudemire's rapid rise from Potential Star to Superstar was due to Nash's deft passing; D'Antoni's run-at-all-costs philosophy, which enabled the tireless Stoudemire to leave his opponents breathing his fumes; or the young man's own limitless athleticism seemed not to matter. He, Nash, and Marion would be the talented troika that would bring Phoenix the championship it had been looking for since Jerry Colangelo brought the franchise into the NBA in 1968.

And now that vision is on hold.

D'Antoni, Marc Iavaroni, and Phil Weber are pondering the Stoudemire news during the twenty-minute ride from the Westin to the University of Arizona. Alvin Gentry, Dan D'Antoni, Todd Quinter, and Noel Gillespie, the young video guru, ride in another car. These twice-daily trips have been, for me, one of the highlights of camp. Weber drives; D'Antoni rides shotgun; Iavaroni and I are in the back. A radio station sends out classic rock, just soft enough that we can criticize the tunes while at the same time singing along. Nonstop conversation, pierced with insults, is the real soundtrack.

But tonight there is a grim, anxious feeling. No Stoudemire for at least four months is the early medical prognosis. No twenty-six points a game for at least four months. No rim-rattling dunks for at least four months. D'Antoni, on whom the major responsibility falls to figure out how to compensate, says: "We just have to make the playoffs." It becomes his mantra. *We just have to make the playoffs.* Eighty-two games and six months lie ahead but *We just have to make the playoffs.*

"The injury is going to throw kind of a wet blanket over the entire town," says Iavaroni.

I ask D'Antoni how he plans to tell the team. He hasn't really thought about it.

"I'll probably talk to each of them individ . . . nah, I'll probably tell them together."

"Word spreads fast," says Iavaroni, "so they'll all know anyway."

D'Antoni chuckles when he thinks of Bryan Colangelo, the Suns' general manager, who drafted Stoudemire and who will undoubtedly be the one to deconstruct the entire situation—repeatedly—to Sarver. Owner and general manager have a tenuous relationship to begin with and this won't help it. "B's probably got his feet hanging over a cliff," says D'Antoni.

The coaches throw out tidbits about how to deal with the injury.

"Shawn's just gotta be a monster," says D'Antoni. "He has to get out there and get his shots. We have to get three-point shooting from our four spot [power forward]. He's gotta knock 'em down."

"We gotta get one more runner," says Weber. "One more guy to join the pack."

"I don't think there's a lot of real good fives [centers] walking around," says D'Antoni. "We more or less got who we got."

"Pat Burke can run," says Weber. "I just wish he'd start making his shot." Burke is a six-foot-eleven-inch, 250-pound left-hander who signed as a free agent in August. There hasn't been much thought about him . . . until now.

"Training camp four years ago in Miami, Mike, we heard about

Zo's kidney," says Iavaroni. "Pat Riley got 'em all together and we won 50 games. You can use it as a rallying cry." Iavaroni was speaking of his time in Miami when the Heat learned that star player Alonzo Mourning was retiring because of kidney disease. He later returned.

"I still think we can score 108, 109, or 110 points," says D'Antoni. That is the way he thinks: When trouble hits, outscore the opposition. When all else fails, amp up the offense. When that fails, amp it up again. "If we can hold up emotional-wise and endurance-wise, if Kurt Thomas stays healthy, if Brian Grant stays healthy, we can surprise a lot of people," says the coach.

We arrive at the University of Arizona's McKale Center just as the other coaches get there. "Well, Alvin, you coached the Clippers," says D'Antoni to Gentry, "what do we do now?"

D'Antoni has decided to tell the team collectively about Stoudemire. His speech is breezy and direct. "I guess most of you guys know about Amare'. Looks like the best it can be is that he's out a month. Or he could be out six months. So we don't know yet and won't until he has all his opinions in. So we just have to band together right now and get it done another way. I don't have any doubts whatsoever. Just make sure you take care of yourself. Get in your extra shooting, talk to Aaron right away if something comes up medically. Because you know what? We have to find a way to score 110 points. We have plenty here to do it, but we gotta find a different way than we did last year. So let's band together and go bust somebody's ass and get it done."

At each break in practice, the coaches gather together and discuss the Stoudemire injury, always facing the stark mathematical reality of replacing twenty-six points per game. (And the secret hope was that Stoudemire would up his average to near thirty without becoming more of a gunner.) Should Marion be more of a post-up player? Should Nash increase his scoring as he did in the previous season's playoffs when, against Dallas, he went for forty-nine points in a single game? Should they work on getting more offense out of Raja Bell, a shooting guard, who was brought in mostly for defense and overall toughness?

Practice is spirited but ragged, and the question hangs in the air: How do we get to 110 without Amare'?

A general atmosphere of optimism permeates the franchise on a surface level. Stoudemire's return date of "sometime around the All-Star Game," which is on February 18, is never confirmed by the medical staff (they know too much can happen) but it seems to be the going gospel anyway. The athlete is presented as a "tireless worker" who, as Nelson says, "would be down here all the time unless we watch him." Doc Carter says the defect in Stoudemire's knee is a centimeter, "which in the realm of things is very small."

But no matter what everyone says, dark thoughts creep in. Similar knee injuries, to NBA stars such as Penny Hardaway and Chris Webber, are dire precedents since neither player was the same after his procedure. And everyone wonders how Stoudemire will react to such a setback early in his career, one that calls for mental toughness. Stoudemire has come very far, very fast. But considering where he came from, doubts about where he is going are always present.

Yes, he is gifted with physical abilities that 99 percent of the world's population can only dream about—a six-foot-ten-inch body, strength, endurance, quickness, a thirty-six-inch vertical leap—but those gifts can't erase the heartache and shame he must've felt at least some of the time when he was growing up. There is so much that he missed, so many things that he'll never know.

His father, Hazell, died when he was twelve. He grew up hand-to-mouth poor, raised by his mother, Carrie, in a drug-infested neighborhood in Lake Wales, just south of Orlando. An older brother, Hazell Jr., ended up in prison on drug and sexual abuse charges. Amare' attended six high schools in five years. It would take two pages to cover Carrie Stoudemire's legal troubles—and should carry the caveat that at least some of the time she was trying to provide for her family—but they include arrests for drugs, prostitution, probation violation, and DUI.

Stoudemire seems almost desperate in his attempt to be a good person and has turned to scripture. He reads the Bible ("Proverbs," he said, "it's my favorite"), and the tattoos that compete for space on his body include Matthew 20:16 ("God bless the child") and the painting of Jesus and the footprints. ("That took four hours," he says, "and it hurt.") On the other hand, the tat that runs in script on his left arm bears a more secular message: "I was raised in this society and this is how you can expect me to be. I do what I want to do." He wrote that passage himself. And to a large extent, Stoudemire *does* do what he wants to do. If you rented a large ballroom and invited in all the professional athletes for whom self-absorption is the default sensibility, you wouldn't have room for a card table. But space would have to be found for Stoudemire. He wants the Suns to win, of course, but he needs to be the star.

Even last season, when he was tearing up the league, his teammates wondered about his commitment to team ball, and their affection for Stoudemire is not of a set piece. But there is a certain collective feeling that, hey, none of us made it here real easily, either, dude, so get your shit together. Marion had some of the same physical gifts, but he, too, overcame a hard life with a single mother who worked her hands to the bone trying to make it right for Shawn and his siblings. He told me one day that he almost never laces up a new pair of sneakers when he doesn't conjure up a memory of going to school in old hand-me-downs, "ratty, worn through, socks all wet, sneakers all wet, feet all wet." Eddie House grew up in a two-parent family, but nobody gave him anything, either. "I knew from early on that I needed a college scholarship to get anywhere," House says, "so I worked my butt off to get better at this game." Nash had domestic stability, but he had to work ten times harder—maybe a *hundred* times harder—than Stoudemire did. The odds on a normal-sized Canadian

Caucasian becoming a two-time MVP aren't even calculable. On it goes. No one gets a pass into the NBA.

But Stoudemire's nightmares with his mother go on. In July of 2004 she was charged with shoplifting more than $1,100 in clothes from a Neiman Marcus in Scottsdale. Some say that she is a good person at heart and that many of her mistakes were made while she was trying to dig out herself and her children from dire circumstances. That would be the first thing I would say about Amare', too—he's a good person. But he's still running hard from his past, and a man doesn't necessarily run any faster because he has a $73 million contract. Sometimes it slows him down.

CHAPTER THREE

[The Second Season]

Los Angeles, April 28 . . . .
SERIES TIED 1–1

"Around here, it's Steve this and Amare' that. What people forget is that I had to adjust my game to different people."

The friend Phil Weber has brought along to the morning coaches meeting in D'Antoni's suite in the Loews Santa Monica Hotel looks familiar. Weber introduces him as "Jim." It doesn't dawn on me who he is until Mike asks him what film projects he's been working on.

"I was gonna say, 'You look like the guy,' " I tell him, "except you *are* the guy." It's Jim Caviezel, the actor who played, most famously, Jesus in Mel Gibson's controversial *The Passion of the Christ*. He and Weber met years ago when Weber was working out players at UCLA and Caviezel was an avid pickup player.

"He gets that a lot," says Weber.

"I feel confident now," says Alvin Gentry. "Phil Jackson doesn't have Jesus sitting in his meeting."

"Phil's probably got some Eastern guy in a white robe," says Iavaroni. "Advantage, Suns."

The mood changes quickly. The Lakers' 99–93 win in Game 2 two nights earlier in Phoenix had put a dark cast on the series, the presence of the Son of God notwithstanding. Nash had played well with twenty-nine points, but, with the exception of Bell, who had twenty-three, everyone else pretty much disappeared, Shawn Marion most conspicuously. Marion had thirteen points (only two in the first half), while the man he was most responsible for checking, Odom, had an active game, making nine of his twelve shots.

A graver concern is that Marion has gone into the tank, or at least stuck one foot into it, partly because news has leaked out that Nash has won his second straight Most Valuable Player award. Marion legitimately likes Nash, and, at some level, recognizes his greatness. Marion never openly challenges Nash's primacy within the team and seems to have accepted his own role as a kind of vice president. When he is critical of the ways the Suns are playing, he generally leaves Nash out of it. "I could be under the basket by myself and don't nobody pass or want to push the ball," Marion complained to Paul Coro of the *Arizona Republic* late in December. "Steve's the only one pushing it. He can't do it by himself."

Still, Marion sees himself as every bit as valuable to the Suns as Nash, and, further, his people around him, in particular his agent, Dan Fegan, see him the same way. During the regular season, Fegan had lobbied with D'Antoni to include Marion in any MVP conversations with the press. Over the next couple of weeks, D'Antoni did exactly that. Yet voters, taking note of his limited ball-handling skills and inability to get off his own shot, don't see him that way at all—only one of 127 MVP voters had Marion in their top five.

His delicate psyche is never far from the coaching staff's collective mind. On the one hand, Marion is outwardly confident, cocky even, buying into that wonderful nickname, Matrix, given to him by TNT commentator Kenny Smith early in Marion's rookie year. The special-effects-driven movie was hot then, and "Matrix" was perfect for a player with an uncanny ability to suddenly materialize in the middle of a play (Marion seems to come from nowhere when he makes a steal, grabs a rebound or makes a quick cut to the basket) and leap from a standing start as if he's on a trampoline. Sometimes Marion refers to himself as the Matrix, as if he has bought into the idea that he is a superhero who defies normal physical laws. His team-mates call him "Trix."

On the other hand, Marion lives in a perpetual state of fear that he is being overlooked, underrespected, ignored, dissed, persecuted, singled out, patronized, whatever. He grew testy with Dan Bickley of the *Arizona Republic* when the columnist asked him about past playoff failures. (Specifically, his 7.8 points-per-game average when San Antonio's Bruce Bowen locked him up in last year's Western finals.) Back in January, Marion told reporters that, in regards to the Olympic team, "Jerry hadn't asked me." At that time, stories were beginning to filter out about which players Colangelo was inviting to the summer tryouts in Las Vegas. Marion was clearly upset; Colangelo was clearly stupefied and came over to resolve it at a practice session.

"Do you remember we talked about the Olympic team last May?" said Colangelo. "During the Dallas series?"

"I remember that," says Marion, "but, you know, I read about the formal interviews and stuff going on and we haven't done that."

"All right, Shawn, look at me," says Colangelo. "Are you in?"

"Yep," says Marion, breaking into a smile.

"Good." And they shake hands.

The Colangelos have always been strong supporters of Marion—it was Bryan who squelched any franchise talk of trading Marion (Sarver wanted to at least entertain the notion when he took over), and it was Bryan who gave him a contract that pays him $13.8 million this season and about $48.6 million through 2009. That is substantially more than Nash, who on his free-agent deal is getting $9.6 million this season and about $34.2 million through 2009. But Marion's view is that no matter how hard he tries, no matter how completely he fills up a box score with points, rebounds, steals, blocked shots, and assists (well, not assists), he cannot gain traction in an organization and a press corps bent on canonizing Nash and anointing Stoudemire as the next superstar.

Even when it works out for Marion ... sometimes it doesn't work out. He went through a streak in late February when he was playing at a level equal to anyone in the league, and D'Antoni, speaking sincerely, carried it a step further, saying that "Shawn Marion, right now, is playing the game as well as anybody ever played it." Marion had scored thirty points and grabbed fifteen rebounds in four consecutive games when D'Antoni, unaware that he was going for five straight, a milestone never previously reached by any Phoenix player, took him out of a safely won game against Milwaukee. When he realized it, D'Antoni hurried him back in. It was awkward, for Marion and both teams, and he missed two shots and one of two free throws to fall one point short.

All this angst gives Marion a certain joylessness from time to time. He really is a good person who should enjoy the game and life a little more than he does. Before a game in New York on January 2, Alvin Gentry was lying on a bench in the locker room, felled by the flu, complaining that he needed something to fill his stomach. As Eddie House waved a bag of greasy chicken fingers over Gentry's nose, Marion said, "See, Alvin, that's what you get when you take three Viagra in one night." Even Gentry laughed.

The day after a home game against the Cleveland Cavaliers on January 14, one the Suns had won 115–106, I asked Marion for his thoughts on the game. "Man," he said, "I don't know what it looked like for you guys. But it was a fun, fun game to be in, you know what I mean?" I did know what he meant. It had been a fun game, an outstanding game, and I was glad that Marion felt that joy. Maybe he feels it more than he shows. A more tender Marion moment came in early February, when, before practice, he suddenly blurted out to his teammates, "I want to thank you all for treating my family nice when they were out here." Marion is extremely close to his mother, Elaine, who was just fourteen when she gave birth to Shawn and his fraternal twin, Shawnett. Two children followed, and Elaine worked two jobs to raise her children. "She did everything for me," says Marion, who does not speak of his father other than to say that he was "recently released from prison." Whenever D'Antoni gets exasperated with Marion, he usually ends up saying: "But Shawn is such a good guy at heart. A really good guy."

There is also a charming naiveté about Marion. He chows down on Hamburger Helper and doesn't care who knows about it. He's an avid cartoon watcher. He's a little, well, thrifty. He favors Holiday Inn Express when traveling on his own dime. One day we were having a conversation about the advantages of having kids close together and Marion pointed to what he considered the key factor—the savings on baby clothes. During his annual pilgrimage to Friedman's, the Atlanta shoe store that caters to large-footed jocks, Marion spent thousands of dollars, then complained about the $17 it cost to mail them. One day last year, one of the trainers was thumbing through a luxury car magazine and musing about making a six-figure auto purchase.

"Why don't you just buy it?" asked Marion.

"Shawn, how much money you think I make?"

"I don't know," said Marion. "Two, three hundred thousand?"

(That is reminiscent of the comment made by Darius Miles, a young player for the Portland Trail Blazers, after he heard that a player had been fined $300,000. "My mother would have to work over a year to make that kind of money," said Miles.)

The question is: Does Marion have a point about being treated unfairly?

A minor one, perhaps.

"I mean, damn, I'm doing things in this league nobody else is doing," Marion had told me a couple of days before the Laker series began. "Come on, now give me my respect. I'm not no big man. I'm a basketball player out here doing things at my size that no one else is doing."

Marion has his defenders around the league. "You can say what you want about Nash and Stoudemire, both great players," Indiana Pacers coach Rick Carlisle said during the season, "but Shawn Marion's ability to run the floor at breakneck speed forces you to play their game. He's more important than anybody knows. If you don't run with him, he goes ahead and dunks it. Or somebody has to pick him up who shouldn't be guarding him, like a guard, and that leaves the three-point line open."

Marion's constant complaint is that, at a lean six-foot-seven inches and 215 pounds, he is frequently asked to defend against players who are much taller, wider, and more physical. (And though he doesn't mention it—but is probably thinking it—the Suns sometimes have to hide Nash on defense.) Marion desperately wants to be known as a "3," a small forward, generally the most athletic player on a team, rather than a "4," a power forward, generally a bigger and slower player. What the coaches want to communicate to Marion is that going against bigger players, filling the power forward spot, is precisely what has *made* him an All-Star. He can use his speed, quickness, and leaping ability to leave other fours in the dust, whereas, against the typical small forward, some of his athleticism would be negated.

I ask Marion if he's happy in Phoenix. He says he is. He even feels that it was "my destiny to be here." While playing in a junior college tournament in Mesa, Arizona, a decade ago, Marion took a side trip to watch the Suns play and got a chance to take one shot on the court. "It was a three-pointer," says Marion, still smiling at the memory, "and it went in. First NBA three-point shot I ever took. I thought, 'This is where I want to be.' " He was elated when the Suns made him the ninth pick of the 1999 draft.

"But, still, there are certain things I can control, certain things I can't," he says. "The things I'm doing now are the things I've been doing since I've been here, before anybody got here." It hurts him that he has never been The Man in Phoenix. Jason Kidd was The Man, then Stephon Marbury was The Man, then Nash became The Man the moment he showed up in the summer of 2004. There have always been other Hamlets, while Marion has been consigned to the role of Rosencrantz or Guildenstern. Worse, Stoudemire, before his injury, seemed to have settled into Second Man status behind Nash, leaving Marion as the Third Wheel. After he was selected as an All-

Star reserve, Marion said, "Ever since I've been in Phoenix, I tried to make myself the face of the Suns on and off the court. That's what it's all about." But he is not the face of the Suns. Nash and D'Antoni are the dual faces, and, whenever Marion's face appears, Stoudemire's is likely to, also. That drives him crazy. He appreciates Nash and gets along with him, but he doesn't feel the same about Stoudemire.

"Around here, it's Steve this and Amare' that," says Marion. "What people forget is that I had to adjust my game to different people. I had J-Kidd. I had Steph. Now I have Steve. All of them are different. I made the adjustments. You got to give me credit now. Don't overlook that.

"The other thing is, people judge players on points. And I think that's wrong." That is obviously directed toward Stoudemire.

During the season, Marion was angry that his likeness didn't appear among the huge bobblehead dolls in the Suns' team store in the arena—the featured ones, of course, were of Nash and Stoudemire. During a couple of regular-season games, a drum line of young men performed during time-outs, all wearing replica jerseys of either Nash or Stoudemire. No Marion. He noticed. It sounds trivial to be complaining about that kind of stuff, particularly when you're compensated as a maximum player, but Marion had a point. There is Stoudemire, not even active, clowning around on the bench, and there is Marion trying to defend Lamar Odom, and yet Stoudemire gets all the love from the drum line. For all the bravado and posturing in the NBA, it is a breeding ground for insecurity.

Marion is also distressed that he doesn't have more of a national profile, both on and off the court. Stoudemire, in street clothes, got more All-Star fan votes than Marion did this season. Marion's main endorsement is with the Room Store in Phoenix, a deal that supplies him with furniture for his mansion in Scottsdale, and the commercial Marion did for the store loops endlessly on local television. He isn't one of Nike's main men, but he does have a signature sneaker, and his swoosh commercial—which was quite good; it showed Marion dominating a pickup game while wearing a weighted vest—ran often during the regular season on national TV. None of the Suns, in fact, Nash and Stoudemire included, are big-time endorsement figures.

Feeling dissed is a common malady in the NBA; the issue is, how does a player react to it? Marion, when feeling undervalued, sometimes gets inspired and sometimes goes into a funk, which is what the staff doesn't want to happen in the remaining games of the series. Two Marion problems had emerged from Game 2. The first is that he wanted to stay, in Iavaroni's words, "hooked" to Lamar Odom. "A certain situation came up in a huddle and I said, 'Okay, Shawn, just switch,' " says Iavaroni. "And he says, 'No, I want to stay on him.' " That is a frequent problem coaches face when trying to communicate the importance of team defense and shared responsibility. A player might come off his man to double-team or trap another player—Marion is adept at that part of the game when motivated—but then get ripped in the press if his man scores a lot of points.

The coaches also have to figure out how to get Marion running on every play, on every turn from defense to offense. Matrix in full flight is the Suns' most potent weapon. But Marion, who averaged forty minutes per game during the regular season (five more than Nash), argues that he can't always run if he's under the defensive basket wrestling with giants. Marion is fond of mentioning that D'Antoni rarely calls a set play for him, and that he needs to get his points "in the flow of the game," as he said after the depressing Game 2 loss. This ignores the fact that the Diaw-to-Marion backdoor lob is probably the "settest" play in the Suns' arsenal.

There are other worries, or, rather, just a kind of undefined, general one. The Suns didn't play well, really, in either of the two games. Their offense, in fact, has really not played well since they scored seventy-two points in the second half to thump Sacramento in a statement game on April 11. Bryant has not yet taken over, which he might decide to do at home in the Staples Center, and the Suns perhaps won't be able to weather it. Each coach deals with the uncertainty in his own way, Iavaroni digging into his personal vault of defensive schemes, D'Antoni latching on to his personal credo that "We're not scoring because we're not pushing," Dan insisting that it's all about effort and will. "I don't think we came out in Game 2 and played like you should in a playoff game," he says. "We didn't come out and say, 'Fuck you.'"

"That's it," says Iavaroni, endlessly searching for the perfect phrase to tell the team. "We have to get back the fuck-you factor."

As the morning shootaround gets underway at the Staples Center, Marion spies Jim Caviezel, sitting courtside.

"Hey, I know you," he says, shyly.

"I'm an actor," says Caviezel.

Marion smiles. "I'm an actor, too."

"Yes, he is," says Iavaroni. "And in the role of the Matrix . . ."

"I loved you in that," says Caviezel.

Marion positively beams. Most athletes quickly learn now to adopt a superior attitude to the public at large, but they still turn into little kids in the presence of movie stars. Stoudemire, on hand as a spectator, edges over to Caviezel during practice and talks to him for fifteen minutes, no doubt positioning himself as a future action hero. "Black Jesus meets White Jesus," says Iavaroni. (Stoudemire has a "Black Jesus" tat on his neck.)

During the film session, Gentry, the pro's pro, sits by Marion, clarifying points from time to time, but mainly just letting him know that the coaching staff is still behind him.

Later, at a restaurant near the hotel, Jesus doesn't make the check disappear, but he does buy lunch.

It's thirty minutes before game time at the Staples Center and nobody looks overly nervous. Perhaps it's an act. In trying to figure out what mentality they should adopt, the Suns finally decided upon "loose," having concluded after Game 2 that they had, according to Eddie House, "lost that carefree attitude they had during the season." Gentry emerges from the wings meeting, doing the that's-right-I'm-bad walk that Richard Pryor and Gene Wilder did in *Stir Crazy*. Stoudemire, who was born in Lake Wales, Florida, and whose favorite team is Florida State, and James Jones, who graduated from the University of Miami, are engaged in a spirited debate over which school has sent the superior talent to the NFL, going through it on a position-by-position basis. If Stoudemire is able to devote half that degree of attention to the rudiments of defense, the Suns will be a much superior team next season.

D'Antoni's main message is to be offensive-minded:

"Okay, guys, catch and shoot. Catch and drive. Dribble-ats. Spread the floor. Attack, Spread the floor. They do have a habit of touching the ball and messing with it. [He means that after the Lakers score they sometimes catch the ball or bat it away to keep the Suns from quick-breaking.] We'll try to bring it to the refs' attention, but you should just grab it and get running. Okay, Noel."

That is the signal for Noel Gillespie to turn on the video. Last season D'Antoni came upon the ploy of ending every pregame session with a minute or so of high-octane Suns' offense. Every possession ends in a basket. The players watch raptly. They can never get enough of their own success.

"This is when we're at our best," says D'Antoni as the video runs, "when we're changing ends on the fly. They have no answer for it. Kwame is awful. Odom's a very average defender. Vujacic [backup point guard Sasha Vujacic] can't guard anybody. And Bryant in the open floor takes chances that aren't good. Let's go get 'em."

The coaches retreat to the small office. Like many arenas around the NBA, the Staples Center devoted little money to the visitor's dressing room. Suddenly, from out in the hallway, comes the voice of Nash.

"NINETEEN ON THE CLICKETY!"

The "clickety" is Nash's word for the clock that clicks off the time until tip-off. Lately, he has taken to loudly shouting out the minutes, screaming it in fact, partly as a joke but also to get his team-mates to follow him onto the court to warm up. Those sports movies in which a team comes charging out of the dressing room together? It doesn't work that way in the NBA. Players drift out in drips and drabs and finally congregate outside the door where they then shout out some sort of war chant and trot onto the floor.

"There's four on the clickety," says Weber to the other coaches. "We better get going."

The game could hardly begin worse for the Suns. In the first minute, Luke Walton knocks Tim Thomas to the floor as he drives, picking up a flagrant foul. Thomas glares at Walton for a moment, and, predictably, several players move toward the action under the basket. From outside the pack, Bryant pushes Diaw, who falls into Smush Parker. Eddie F. Rush, a veteran referee, calls a technical on Diaw.

"Eddie, Eddie, did you see it?" D'Antoni pleads with Rush. "Boris never pushes anybody. He didn't do it. He got pushed."

"I saw what I saw," Rush tells him.

"But did you see the push?" D'Antoni says.

"I saw what I saw."

A few minutes later, Diaw is hit with the obligatory three-second defensive call, which results in an automatic technical foul shot. It's like a little beeper from the league office goes off during the first period of every game, reminding officials to make the call, after which they will ignore the defensive three-second call the rest of the way since virtually none of the spectators—and only half of the players—understand it.

In the third quarter, Bell gets elbowed by Kwame Brown, and, in an ensuing scrum, Diaw falls. Brown is whistled for a technical foul. But then Brown stands over Diaw, his crotch somewhere over Diaw's midsection, and glares down at him. Perhaps Brown is still trying to prove something to his coach; earlier in the season, Jackson had called him a "sissy." Jackson said he didn't mean it like it sounded, but it resonated for Brown, who had been called a "faggot" by Michael Jordan, who drafted him when he was a Washington Wizards executive, then torched him when he was a Wizards player.

Brown's action is exactly the kind of thug behavior the NBA is trying to curtail, but no technical foul is called. Nash moves toward the action, and, in the process, pushes away Vujacic's arm. Bryant then trots over to Nash and they jaw at each other. Later in the third period, Bryant is called for a foul on a blocked shot attempt and, irritated, walks away, lifting his jersey over his head in front of another veteran referee, Bill Spooner. Spooner tells him, "Put your jersey down."

Clearly, L.A. is trying to punk a team it considers punk-able. The Lakers never really run away and hide, but they seem in control, calm even. When Bell is whistled for fouling Bryant with 4:18 left, he explodes in anger and draws a technical foul. Then D'Antoni, rushing to support him, gets one, also, the second and third T's the Suns have received. Leandro Barbosa's layup brings Phoenix to within 92–90 with 3:28 left, but Walton and Parker score consecutive baskets and the Lakers go on to win 99–92.

It is the nightmare scenario presented by Iavaroni. Bryant scored only seven points, but every other starter was in double figures. Kobe played the role of Prospero, directing everything, seeing all, being all, and acting quite superior about it all. D'Antoni decides on a psychological ploy, telling the media that Bell has done a great job subduing Kobe. Perhaps that will rile up the Laker and precipitate a shooting spree that will freeze out his teammates.

But with a 2–1 series deficit and Game 4 on the road, reality has set in: The Suns are two losses from an ignominious first-round exit.

CHAPTER FOUR

[The Second Season]

Los Angeles, April 29 . . . .
LAKERS LEAD SERIES 2–1

> *"If you get a reputation as a punk-ass team—and that's what we are right now—it's one of the worst things that can happen."*

It's 7:30 a.m., and Steve Nash can't sleep. He leaves his wife, Alejandra, and adorable twin daughters, Lola and Bella, upstairs, grabs a towel, and heads downstairs, where he runs into D'Antoni. It goes without saying that the coach hadn't slept either. He rolled around for most of the night, pizza and diet soda in his gut from a postgame video review, the horror of a 2–1 deficit on his mind, anger building about what he perceives as inept officiating. So the two of them relax in the back lobby of the Loews Hotel in Santa Monica, the still, blue waters of the Pacific visible through the wide picture windows behind them. Nash had been on his way for an ocean dip, in fact, when he encountered D'Antoni. Nash figured the ocean wouldn't be any colder than his daily restorative ice bath and would afford him time to think. Anyway, he's Canadian.

They are comfortable with each other, as comfortable as player can be with coach. Without talking about it, they understand what one has done for the other, Nash getting a coach who will let him dribble-probe, D'Antoni getting a point guard who can implement his unselfish, play-quick system. They even joke around with each other, which doesn't happen much given the delicate psyches that prevail in pro sports. A couple of times during the season, after Nash had a big scoring first quarter then turned to his inevitable role of distributor, he would throw a jersey across the locker room in mock anger after the game. "Frickin' D'Antoni got me out of my game!" When Nash was named Canada's athlete of the year, D'Antoni said to him, "That's a great honor, Steve. Did you beat out one of those curling guys who sweep the ice?"

Player and coach talk for a half hour about a lot of things, neither of them coming to any definitive conclusions about the series outside of the reality that the Suns have to get tougher. They are getting bullied, pushed around, maybe even intimidated by the Lakers. Nash will admit to being a little tired and concedes that he is having a hard time getting around Kwame Brown when a pick-and-roll produces a switch.

"We have to keep diving," says Nash. When the Suns' offense is at its best, there is constant movement off the ball. Nash dribbles and probes, probes and dribbles, and the other Suns make quick cuts—dives—to the basket. What sometimes happens, though, is that his teammates stand around and watch him, like it's a halftime exhibition, and if Nash can't get by his man, the offense stagnates. It's not always the fault of the others, though. If Nash is stopped far from the basket, and two taller defenders are putting up a wall around him, he simply cannot see over them. Players can dive all they want, but it will be for naught. Still, it's a percentage game, as Nash sees it. He considers his greatest strength to be finding open men while he's dribbling, but it's mandatory that he find them on the move.

At the end of the conversation, Nash asks D'Antoni, with a charming earnestness: "You don't believe in those conspiracy theories, do you?" Conspiracy theories in the NBA are nothing new. Pro basketball has always had such a tenuous hold on the American public that there is the perception in some quarters that the league must, well, *guide* the fortunes of the postseason into the most attractive matchups. And the only way to guide is through the officiating. The most attractive matchups are always about personalities, and, while the hard-core NBA fan is likely to appreciate the Suns as much as any team—the up-tempo play, the unselfishness, the ball distribution, the lightning-quick air strikes of the Matrix, the creative abilities of Nash—the casual fan thirsts for Kobe Bryant, a *personality.* The farther the Lakers advance in the playoffs, the more Bryant; the more Bryant, the higher the TV ratings. And if the Lakers could somehow emerge as the Western Conference champion, and the Miami Heat could come out of the East, the Finals would amount to a reality show pitting Bryant against Shaquille O'Neal, onetime Laker teammates who are now adversaries. America would *understand* that.

"Nah, I don't believe that, Steve," says D'Antoni. "We'll get some whistles tomorrow night. We'll go spank 'em, get this thing tied up, get home and get right."

Robert Sarver is waiting with the assistants in front of D'Antoni's suite. Even after their one-hour postgame video review, the coaches had been up for much of the night. Weber fell asleep sitting up, awakening to find that his pen had drawn a jagged line through his notes. Iavaroni is almost apologetic as he confesses that he had done a poor job of analysis. "I was too emotionally invested last night," he says. "I felt like I was dying after that game. I'll do better this morning." Sarver had gotten only a little more sleep but he is fired up.

"This L.A. bullshit has got to stop," said the owner. Right before the tip-off of last night's game he was incensed to see actress/director Penny Marshall, a long-time NBA fan, near the Suns' huddle, talking to some of the players. "I already told Tucker [team security director Kevin Tucker] that that bullshit stops on Sunday. This is war!" To no one in particular, he says, of the Lakers: "I hate those guys."

The time has come for toughness. Or, at least, tough talk. As the coaches once again review Game 3—it doesn't look any more palatable than it did seven hours earlier—they alternate between being furious at the officiating and furious at how placidly their players have been in dealing with the Lakers' aggressiveness. Aside from Nash getting into it briefly with Bryant, the Suns have been cast in the role of Curly, the Stooge who gets fingered in the eye and conked on the head and accepts it all.

"I tell you what," says Gentry, "if you get a reputation as a punk-ass team—and that's what we are right now—it's one of the worst things that can happen."

On screen, there's a scramble for a loose ball late in the game, and the Lakers pounce on it. Gentry becomes animated.

"After all that happened, don't you just . . ."

"I think you drive his fucking head into the ground," says D'Antoni.

"Thank you," says Gentry.

"Whose head are you talking about?" I ask.

"Any of their heads," says Gentry. "Obviously, Raja would do it. But they know he's watching them."

Indeed, a couple weeks earlier, Bell had been awakened by a call from the NBA, warning him that he would be closely watched in the playoffs for prior acts of aggression. Such warnings are not unprecedented, and the NBA considers them to be a favor. The Suns prefer to think of Bell as being on "double secret probation," as the brothers of Delta House were in *Animal House*.

Sarver relishes this kind of talk. He was never much of a basketball player—his sports are tennis and golf—but his no-nonsense business personality and general feistiness suggest the kind of bulldog who would knock his opponent down, then step on him as he headed back in the other direction.

"So, in other words, if a guy has a layup, instead of just patting him on the back, you should knock him down so he can't make it?" asks Sarver, warming to the subject.

The problem is, as the coaches explain, with the exception of Bell and Kurt Thomas (who is on the shelf with a foot injury), the Suns are not naughty by nature.

"Eighteen years in the NBA and I can tell you this: It's either in you or it's not," says Gentry.

"So you can't just appoint somebody to do it?" asks Sarver, sounding disappointed.

"No," says Gentry. "If we were going to do it, we would've done it last night after Kwame stood over Boris, punking him. We wouldn't have had to say anything. Next time down it goes into Kwame and he laid it in for a three-point play, that right there, somebody would've taken him down. Raja would've done it, but he knows they're watching. Coaches don't have to tell you to do those things, you just do them."

"In all fairness to us," says Sarver, "we knew we had a certain lack of toughness last year and we addressed it. We got Raja. We got Kurt, who should be in there. Amare' should be in there."

Sarver's presence is not taken as unusual or discomfiting by the coaches. It might've been last year when he was just learning the ropes and seemed to have a knack for saying and doing the wrong thing, such as flapping his arms like a chicken at the San Antonio bench when Spurs coach Gregg Popovich decided to rest an injured Tim Duncan. But now it seems like he's honestly trying to learn the game.

But his curve is stiff. Jerry Colangelo, the man against whom Sarver will be eternally compared, was unique as an owner in that he was a player, a coach, a general manager, and a scout. Colangelo also chaired the NBA's competition and rules committee for many years. "The game itself," Colangelo says, "is everything to me." The game is not everything to Robert Sarver and never will be. The important thing is that he not suddenly start recommending lineup changes or suggesting defenses to apply on Kobe.

"You know what?" says Gentry. "If we have Amare' in this series, he rolls down the lane, gets the ball, dunks on Kwame Brown's head, and next thing you know Kwame Brown is sitting over there on that bench."

There is also the problem of *how* to fire someone up. Should a coach get in Marion's face and scream at him that he *must* knock down Odom? Would that be effective? There is a reaction to every action. Sarver is transfixed by this, stupefied by the coaches' attention to psychological detail. He lets them know that by his high-pitched laugh.

"Hey, Robert, in this business you have to be careful," says Iavaroni. "A guy will go into an absolute funk if he feels you're beating him up."

"It's the exact opposite of how the regular business world works," says Sarver. "You try to be sensitive to the people who make the least money because they're not getting paid necessarily to do it right. But the guy who's making three, four hundred grand, he's the guy you come down with the hammer on."

"Does he have a five-year guaranteed contract?" asks Iavaroni with a smile.

Sarver laughs. "Hey, I'm not saying it's wrong. I'm just saying it's bizarre. Okay, hang in there, guys."

There is a feeling of quiet desperation in the room. Down 2–1 on the road. Make a drastic change on offense or defense? Iavaroni returns to the theme with which he began the series: Get Kobe shooting, which will get the others watching.

"I know this is a little drastic," says Iavaroni, "but hear me out. How about if we just one-swipe Kobe and let him shoot." "One-swipe" is exactly what it sounds like—a second defender would come over toward Bryant, take a swipe at the ball to (perhaps) discourage penetration, but then return to his man. It would not be a double-team or a trap.

Mike shakes his head. "I'm not there, Marc."

"I'm just searching a little bit," says Iavaroni.

"Well, I don't know whether we should be searching," says D'Antoni. "We should tighten up things, sure, but I think we should get better at what we're doing."

You can tell Iavaroni doesn't agree, but he concedes. "I just want to win the next game," says Iavaroni, "and we're all smart enough to realize that the next game pretty much decides the series."

"No, I'm not there, either," says D'Antoni. "I know what you're saying, but I'm not there. We lose tomorrow? Okay, we win at home. We gotta win the sixth game here. That's it. That's what it comes down to. I understand being down three-to-one is hard. But let's keep doing what we're doing. Give ourselves a chance to win. Give ourselves a chance to get it done. Keep doing what we're doing. I'm not sure we're that far away. We were there last night, as hard as it was to lose. We had our shots to beat them. We had our opportunities."

The room is quiet for a moment. Then D'Antoni speaks again. "I don't think there is a big, grand solution. I just think we have to do a better job of doing what we're doing. We're there. We're there."

I'm not sure D'Antoni really believes it, or keeps saying it just to convince himself. But he is convinced that superior teams win not by panicking or changing schemes but by holding the line and doing what they do best. He decides that the afternoon practice will be simple and will reflect none of the angst being poured out in this morning meeting. "We'll talk about bringing up the ball quickly and being more decisive on offense," says D'Antoni. "Defensively, our schemes are exactly where they need to be. We'll talk about tightening them up and not over-helping."

Comic relief, fortuitously, is supplied when the coaches come to the third-quarter play where Diaw is knocked down and Brown stands over him. The play had brought coaches from both benches onto the court, and, at the side of the frame, here comes Phil Jackson, ambling into view, with his peculiar, pain-ridden, side-to-side gait.

"Look!" says Mike. "It's the Penguin!"

Penguin sounds fill the room for the next minute. That and laughter, which is desperately needed.

CHAPTER FIVE

[The Second Season]

Los Angeles, April 29 . . . .

"After I finished talking to Stu, I think my blood pressure hit three hundred."

The Suns bus to practice at a middle school in Santa Monica, a facility frequently used by teams when they don't want to make the long downtown drive to the Staples Center. No one would know that this is a team in crisis. None of the uncertainty about what to change and how to play and who to guard with whom comes up. D'Antoni gathers them around and says:

"This is something we talked about earlier. You lose one and you never think you're going to win again; you win one, you never think you're going to lose again. We do have to win three games, but we only have to do it one at a time. We can do that starting at 12:30 tomorrow. We win that game and all of a sudden we're coming back with the edge.

"Okay, we lose this game, we go back to Phoenix and win a game, and, again, the pressure's on them. We have to have the mind-set, one possession at a time, one game at a time. Don't let the outside stuff, don't let the papers, don't let anything distract you."

Snippets of the game are shown on the portable video system that Noel Gillespie lugs around on the road in a gigantic orange case. (It looks like something a magician would carry; everyone calls it "Noel's Lady.") The coaches had just spent an hour bemoaning the number of times that the Suns failed to make the extra pass or failed to get a better shot, but they choose only one to show—a play where Marion has both Bell and Barbosa wide-open but instead launches a three-pointer. D'Antoni says, "Be cognizant of the fact that there are times we can swing it."

Practice is short and crisp. The media comes in, looking for a fresh angle on the Suns' obituary that is almost ready to be written, but finds a loose team rather than a desperate one. It could've been the day before a meaningless game against the Charlotte Bobcats in December. Nash shoots alone at one basket while Dan D'Antoni bangs his ear. Phil Weber works with Diaw on his shooting, the Frenchman frowning every time the coach sends him to a new spot but eventually complying. Diaw likes to demand an extra shot when he gets started; instead of a "mulligan," a word that does not exist in French, he calls it a "hooligan." Kurt Thomas is playing a shooting game with Kevin Tucker, the Suns' security man, who played college ball at Northern Arizona. A buzz has begun about the possibility of Thomas returning from his foot injury—everyone in the Suns' camp would pay a week's salary to have Thomas come in and bust Kwame Brown in the chops—but D'Antoni considers it a long shot. "I haven't shot a ball in nine weeks," says Thomas to Tucker, "and I still kicked your ass."

Vinny Del Negro, the Suns' radio analyst and a former NBA player, works with Barbosa on his shooting. Pat Burke and Nikoloz Tskitishvili, "Skita" to everyone, play a spirited one-on-one game. As the playoffs go on, and the likelihood of the eighth through twelfth players actually getting into a game decreases, the ferocity of the scrubs' postpractice battles intensifies. Stoudemire, a pick sticking out from his hair, studies his BlackBerry and relates to James Jones the selections from the ongoing NFL draft.

Eddie House approaches D'Antoni. He isn't sure he should do it, but the coach always seems open to suggestions.

"You know, the bench was a big part of what we did all season," House tells him. "Don't forget about us now." In last night's game, the top six—Nash, Marion, Diaw, Bell, Tim Thomas, and Barbosa—all played thirty or more minutes. Bell played forty-five. But James Jones got in for only eight minutes and House played for only five.

"I appreciate that, Eddie, I really do," says Mike. "And I'm going to think about it. We'll need you down the road. But I have a hard time playing you and Steve together because of how physical they are." What he didn't add was: *We're not cutting Steve's minutes, and we're worried about your ability to handle the ball under pressure.*

Back in the winter months, House had been playing so well that he was an early candidate for the Sixth Man award. He was D'Antoni's torch, instant offense off the bench. One game in particular, against the Denver Nuggets at home on December 2, sums up his contributions. He made five jumpers in a row to pull the Suns out of trouble. On one play the ball was barely in his hands before he got his quick 1-2 pitty-pat steps down and shot it in rhythm. It was the game-clinching three-pointer from the right wing, and, as the Nuggets called time-out to cool him off, House sat down, received high-fives all around, and said, "Fuck those motherfuckers." That is classic Eddie House. *Fuck those motherfuckers.* On at least a half-dozen occasions, his bravado had carried the Suns in those early months; House and his teammates loved it when Noel Gillespie found the scouting report of an opposing team that said this about House: *Won't shoot it unless he has it in his hands.*

But, now, with the playoff noose tightening, Eddie House is just another stray scrounging for scraps.

On the way out of the gym, Gentry sidles up to Boris and says, "Well, another day, another franc." Stoudemire asks, "What's that? Like a French dollar?" Diaw shakes his head as only the French can. "It is the other way around," he tells Stoudemire. "The dollar is the French franc. The franc was around for five hundred years before the dollar." Stoudemire considers this.

• • •

For D'Antoni, the real business of the day—and it is unpleasant business—is calling Stu Jackson, the NBA's director of operations. Jackson, a former player, coach, and general manager, is charged with everything relating to the game itself. During the season, for all intents and purposes, that task boils down to handling team complaints about referees, meting out punishments to players and coaches for technical fouls and flagrant fouls, and—deep below the radar—fining officials for bad calls. While the league announces every dollar taken from a player or coach for bitching about the officials, referee fines are kept in-house.

Any fair-minded individual would have to concede that Jackson has a difficult job, akin to listening to the complaints about the czar from a mob of pissed-off peasants during the Russian Revolution. Jackson's predecessor in the job, by the way, was Rod Thorn, a West Virginian who is now the general manager of the New Jersey Nets. Thorn is a basketball legend in the Mountain State. He followed Jerry West to the state university and was given West's number 44. Four years after Thorn graduated, Mike D'Antoni, a six-foot-three-inch playmaking guard from the mining town of Mullens, was recruited with the understanding that he would wear 44 and continue the line. But D'Antoni opted to play at the state's "other" university, Marshall, where brother Dan had forged a fine career. (West Virginia University recently retired 44 in West's name only, which, as D'Antoni says, "The dumb asses should've done in the first place.")

There is little personal bond between D'Antoni and Jackson, which is how it should be. The worst thing that could happen to Jackson would be the perception that he favors one team over another. On the other hand, the idea that Jackson is an impartial observer is ridiculous. Jackson works for the czar and lives in the palace. He's the Big Chief of the Referees. Asking for judicial relief from Jackson is not unlike the Kafkaesque feeling a college student has when he appeals a suspension handed down by the administration, only to find that the appeals court is the same one that handed out the suspension. Anyway, officials' calls are not reversible in boardrooms. Except for questions about a shot beating the clock, which the refs can review at courtside, calls are set in stone the moment a whistle is blown. The reason coaches and GMs call Jackson to complain, beyond the fact that venting is good for the soul and the blood pressure, is to set the stage for the next game. *Watch out for this.* That is particularly important, obviously, during a protracted playoff series.

Earlier in the season, Jackson happened to be in Phoenix when the Suns lost an agonizing 103–101 game to the Minnesota Timberwolves—the Suns protested that a goaltend should've been called against Kevin Garnett in the final seconds. D'Antoni came into the office, kicked his chair (which sent the height adjustment lever flying), then whipped off his sport coat and heaved it against the wall. "The good news," he said later, "was I managed to lay off the plasma TV." The Suns protested to Jackson, who promised to review the play (though it wouldn't do any good anyway). The next day Jackson came back with his verdict: "Had there been another half-turn on the ball before Garnett blocked it, it would've been a goaltend." Alvin Gentry, who has impeccable comedic timing, said, "They also found a second shooter on the grassy knoll."

D'Antoni places the call to Jackson in the early afternoon. He gets Jackson's answering machine, but Jackson is good about returning calls. D'Antoni states his case:

—The game started badly when Luke Walton flagrantly fouled Tim Thomas, and Diaw was mistakenly called for a technical on the ensuing group grope around the basket. The Suns did nothing and received the same penalty as the Lakers.

—After being hit with a technical for throwing an elbow, Kwame Brown stood over Diaw and glared down at him, essentially putting his crotch over Diaw's face. He should've been assessed another technical and ejected.

—Bryant walked right by referee Bill Spooner and put his jersey over his head to protest a call. That should've been a technical.

—And in a general sense, the Lakers, a much more physical team, are manhandling our players, on and off the ball. Yet, in last night's game, Phoenix shot seventeen free throws and the Lakers shot twenty-three.

At five p.m. D'Antoni comes downstairs, bound for the annual media dinner hosted by public relations chief Julie Fie. No players attend, but D'Antoni has given his commitment. He wishes he hadn't. He looks ashen and shaken. He has a half-smile plastered on his face, but it's one of those dangerous, I-might-kill-somebody smiles. D'Antoni talks animatedly to his brother, then to Gentry. Then he comes over and explains what Jackson said when he called back.

"Stu said he looked at everything and, at the end of the day, he says he's assessing Raja a flagrant-one [the lightest of the flagrant fouls] for a play that happened with four minutes to go in the third period," he says.

"I don't remember the play," I say.

"A rebound gets tapped out, Raja turns and starts to run and Kwame Brown grabs him and holds him for a second, so Raja rips his hand away and his hand hits Kwame in the mouth. That's it. I had to look for the play myself."

"Why would that be a flagrant-one?"

"Stu said that it's the kind of thing that escalates into a fight. He said he even talked to David Stern [the commissioner] about it. He said Raja and Kwame became 'intertwined.' I pointed out that Kwame grabbed him, and that's not the real definition of 'intertwined.'

"Then I went back to the first play and said, 'You're telling me that what Raja did, reacting to a foul that should've been called, is more dangerous than Kobe pushing Boris into the fray?' Stu says, 'I understand that one. We're rescinding the technical on Boris. [Meaning Diaw will not have to pay $1,000, or whatever that is in francs, the standard technical-foul fine.]'

"So let me get this straight. Luke Walton tackles our guy. Kwame

Brown elbows a guy, then puts his crotch over somebody's face. Kobe Bryant lifts his jersey over his head. And I'm walking into my locker room tomorrow and telling my guys that, after all that, they get one technical and one flagrant, and we get one flagrant and three technicals. That's what you got for me? Because I'll tell you right now what the player reaction will be: We're getting screwed. I just want to make sure you're okay with your decision."

D'Antoni says Jackson told him: "I understand you're upset. But that's the decision."

Jackson has his own interpretation of all this, of course. Luke Walton committed a flagrant foul and it was called. Somebody went sprawling in a pack, and the ref did the best job he could to determine who was guilty of a technical; the technical itself cannot be rescinded but the attached fine has been. Not calling technicals on Brown and Bryant are judgment calls. Hitting Bell with a flagrant-one stops a potentially explosive situation; Bell had been previously warned not to be an aggressor. And as for the free-throw discrepancy, well, the refs are calling them the way they see them. Lots of times—maybe even most times—the more aggressive team will get to the foul line more often. There you have it.

The Lakers would have their own interpretation of all this, too: The Suns are whining, and we have them in our hip pocket.

D'Antoni attends the media dinner, almost in a daze. "After I finished talking to Stu," he says, "I think my blood pressure hit three hundred." I urge him to have a glass of red wine instead of his usual Diet Coke. He relates the story of the Jackson phone call to Sarver and Del Negro. He has another glass of wine and a good meal. By the time he takes a cab back to the hotel, he says that, while he hasn't forgotten the spirit-sapping phone call, he is now focused on tomorrow's game.

"These are the times that try men's souls," he says.

"Thomas Paine," I say.

"No," says D'Antoni. "I'm pretty sure it's Phil Jackson."

CHAPTER SIX

[The Second Season]

Los Angeles, April 30 . . . .
LAKERS LEAD SERIES 2–1

"We better have enough edge that it doesn't come down to one shot and number 8 has the ball in his hands."

The quiet of the pregame locker room is spoiled by a cameraman who, while taking a close-up of Eddie House, trips over a bench and falls. "It's NBA-TV, ladies and gentleman," intones Pat Burke. "We're bringing you a live shot of Eddie House's balls."

Burke, a communications major at Auburn, is a very funny guy, though he's gotten a little less humorous and a lot more bitter with the disappearance of his playing time as the season has gone on.

Robert Sarver enters. He is fired up, more fired up, it seems, than the handful of players who are quietly getting dressed.

"Fuck L.A.," he announces. "Fuck Kobe. Fuck these fans. Fuck the refs. Fuck everything. We beat these guys like a drum three times during the season. Let's go out there and kick fucking ass."

A few players murmur assent. Kurt Thomas is talking to his girl-friend on a cellphone. Who was that? she asks.

"Oh, that was our owner," answers Thomas.

Before the game, Paul Coro, the Suns' beat reporter for the *Arizona Republic,* asks Bell for his reaction to the added flagrant 1 he had received from the league office on the play that few people re-member.

"I don't know what you're talking about," says Bell.

D'Antoni had decided not to inform Bell until after the game but forgot to mention that to Coro. Bell shrugs it off. "Guess that mean's they're still watching me," he says.

Iavaroni gathers the bigs together for their meeting. He believes it's the most important meeting of the year, a Game 4 on the enemy court with your team down.

"I wanna tell you a story," he begins. "I don't do it much. It's my first preseason game as a rookie with the 76ers. Nineteen eighty-three. We're playing the Celtics. I'm guarding Larry Bird. I get it inside, turn, and he fouls me. So Bird says to Dennis Johnson, "We got us a bitch here." I turn to D.J. and say, 'Can't he play this bitch without fouling?'

"Well, I got into Bird's head. I could see it and I could hear it. He did nothing but talk the rest of the half, trying to get back at me. And he didn't do that well. But in the second half he just comes out and plays. Somebody tells me later that he scored the first twenty points of the half himself.

"Moral of the story? He was best when he was all business. He wasn't talking. He was concentrating his energies on playing. That's what we have to do today. Take care of business."

Iavaroni calls on Kurt Thomas, as he often does in the bigs meeting. (When Thomas played for Dallas in the 1997–98 season, Don Nelson made him an assistant coach during the time he was injured.) "Kurt," says Iavaroni, "you're one of the best, if not *the* best, post defender I ever saw. Tell us some of the things you kept in your mind when you think about playing a guy one-on-one."

"Stay low," answers Thomas. "Stay centered. Keep your balance. And you have to hit him first once in a while. Don't be afraid to throw in a cheap shot. Hit him with an elbow. Let him know you're there."

That might've been more information than Iavaroni was looking for. But he moves on. "Kwame Brown," says Iavaroni, "is just a big fucking guy who doesn't move much. But you have to adapt to play him. It's origin of the species. Anyone ever hear of a guy named Charles Darwin? You gotta adapt."

D'Antoni is normally a strategist in the general sense. The Suns don't have a lot of set plays, but they do have that philosophy of keeping the ball moving, so he generally just reminds them to use every offensive weapon at their disposal. But tonight he drifts toward the mind game.

"Every possession play with your heart and your mind," he says. "Ignore the refs. Don't let them get into your head. It falls on us. It's not about them. It's not about the Lakers. It's about us. It's about whether we can get it done."

Out on the court, meanwhile, Sarver is putting his fuck-L.A. mind-set into action. He sidles up to Norman Pattiz, the founder of the Westwood One Radio Network and one of those irritating Laker superfans who sit near the bench and scream at any opposing player who happens by that area. Sarver says to him, "You ever touch one of my players again, you'll have me to deal with." Sarver thought he had noticed Pattiz getting into the face of Tim Thomas during Game 3.

"You're an asshole," says Pattiz dismissively.

"I may be an asshole," says Sarver, "but you better understand— you'll have me to deal with."

The game is even through most of the first half, which ends in a 41–41 tie. But it's the kind of *even* that favors the Lakers—the slow tempo, the shaky shooting, the physical play, and, most of all, the fact that Bryant missed eleven minutes of action after getting his third foul. That was the time to capitalize, and the Suns couldn't do it, having been outscored 16–15. It was like getting beat by just the Pips at a talent show.

But the Suns finally wake up in the second half, Marion in particular. They battle for loose balls, turn Parker and Luke Walton into nonfactors, and no longer seem intimidated by Kwame Brown. Nash goes out for his prescribed rest late in the third period, but his problematic back tightens up and he sits out the first couple minutes of the fourth quarter. Still, the Suns stay in control. A trio of dagger three-point shots by Devean George, a perennial Laker underachiever; some emotional play by Sasha Vujacic, who looks like he's going to burst into tears at every call that goes against him ("You suck," Bell calmly informed Vujacic during Game 2); and the overall brilliance of Bryant keep the Lakers close. But with 5:41 left, Bryant forces a shot between two defenders, and, in the ensuing time-out, Lamar Odom remains on the court, pouting, staring at Kobe. The Suns lead 81–73. This is the Iavaroni model: Kobe is trying to take over the game and his supporting cast is angry at him. The *Good Ship Laker* has been turned into *Family Feud*.

But then two straight atrocious calls go against the Suns. Marion cleanly blocks a Bryant shot, but referee Sean Corbin calls a foul. On the previous play, Bryant had "mother-fucked" Corbin, complaining about a noncall—the F-word in some form will usually get you a technical—and the Suns view this as a makeup. On the Lakers' next possession, Odom, in a post-up position, gets the ball and simply barrels over Marion, makes the basket, and, incredibly, gets a foul call, too. He completes the three-point play and, worse, the foul is Marion's sixth, sending him to the bench. He had been the one who had held the Suns together in the second half with fourteen points and seven rebounds.

The one-two punch puts the Lakers back in the game, but, still, the Suns show fortitude and reseize control. With twelve seconds left they lead 90–85. John Black, the Lakers' director of public relations, asks me if I'll be back in L.A. for Game 6; this one is essentially over. I leave my press seat and squeeze in between Dan D'Antoni and Todd Quinter on the Suns' bench. Walking in with the team is the only way I can get access to the locker room before the rest of the press corps.

"This is okay, right?" I ask them.

They look at me nervously but don't say anything.

At that moment, the Lakers inbound the ball, and Smush Parker, the third option on the play, an erratic marksman who had missed his first twelve shots of the game, hits a three-pointer with Nash right in his face to cut the lead to 90–88. D'Antoni and Quinter look at me as if I'd brought with me a case of the Black Plague. The Suns take time-out to plan an inbounds play, D'Antoni giving responsibility for Diaw to get it to Nash. A statistic that has haunted the Suns all season must be in the minds of a few of them: In regular-season games decided by seven points or fewer, the Suns are 0-7. It is hopeless to figure out the logic of that, given the reality of Nash, the ultimate heady quarterback and one of the best foul-shooters in the league.

This play goes badly right away. The Lakers swarm Nash, and Diaw looks anxious. Nash keeps moving toward the pass, trying to shake Parker, and slips just as he receives the pass. Parker is right on top of him and steals the ball. Parker taps it to George, who gets it to Bryant, who takes a few high-speed dribbles and puts up a high-arcing, high-degree-of-difficult layup over the outstretched arm of Diaw. It goes in. Tie game 90–90. I return to my press seat without a word, taking the Plague with me.

D'Antoni designs a brilliant inbounds play that all but frees James Jones for a layup, but he is held by at least two Laker defenders—in those situations, fouls are rarely called—and can't get off a clean shot. Overtime.

Momentum had clearly switched to the Lakers, but the Suns play with guts in the extra period, and when Nash, gritting his teeth in pain (his back had started to hurt him), hits a three-pointer, they lead 98–95 with forty-nine seconds left. The Suns get the ball back but, with the shot clock going down, Bell shoots an air ball. What Phoenix needed was something that would've at least drawn iron, bounced around, killed some clock. But it gives the Lakers a dead-ball situation.

Afraid to foul, the Suns allow Bryant an open lane to the hoop and he scores a layup with 11.7 seconds left to draw the Lakers within one, 98–97. The Suns' plan is obvious: Get it to Nash, one of the surest dribblers and free-throw shooters on the planet. They elect not to take a time-out and inbound from under the Lakers' basket. Probably better that way. More room for Nash to operate.

Nash begins dribbling under pressure and heads toward midcourt, veering left all the while. As it becomes evident he's going to run into a crowd, Diaw calls and motions for a time-out. Nash hollers for one, too, but can't make a hand gesture because he's concentrating too much on his dribble. He gets jostled as Lamar Odom and Luke Walton close in on him. Referees Bennett Salvatore and Kenny Mauer peer in at the play but don't call anything until, finally, Salvatore motions for a jump ball. Walton against Nash.

Brian Grant insists that he heard Diaw calling for a time-out from the bench, which is across the court. The coaches are incensed that the Suns weren't given the time-out or a foul wasn't called. Of the three possible calls in that situation, a jump ball is by far the rarest.

But jump ball it is. The six-foot-eight-inch Walton has the edge on the six-foot-two-inch Nash, and, predictably, taps it back to Bryant with about six seconds to go. It is so predictable that even the press corps wonders why more Phoenix defenders are not grouped around Bryant. He dribbles toward the Laker basket and even then is not as swarmed as he should be. Diaw is closest to him, just as he was on the layup, and, as Bryant goes up for a jumper, I can hear Alvin Gentry's words from the Friday night postgame video review: *I tell you, we better have enough edge that it doesn't come down to one shot and number 8 has the ball in his hands.*

With perfect rotation, the ball goes in, and the home crowd goes nuts. Lakers win 99–98. The moment is instantly sanctified as one of the greatest in Staples Center history, right up there with the Robert Horry jumper that beat the Sacramento Kings in Game 6 of the 2002 Western finals. The Randy Newman song blares: *I love L.A.! I love L.A.!*

The Lakers and their fans are still in wild celebration as the Suns troop funereally to their dressing room. The coaches gather outside, as they always do, but no one has anything substantive to offer. D'Antoni stands with his head down for a full two minutes, and, when it's time to address the team, he has almost nothing to say. "We're going home, guys. We'll get 'em there. A lot of stuff happened. Try to forget about it."

Leandro Barbosa emerges from the shower, a stricken look on his boyish, open face. "Did . . . you . . . ever . . . see . . . anything . . . like . . . that?" he asks, almost as if he's in shock.

"Can't say that I have, L.B," I say.

Dan D'Antoni switches off his cell phone as he walks slowly from the dressing room to the tunnel, where the team bus is waiting to take them to the airport and on to Phoenix. "I feel like a hundred years old," he says, limping, a badly swollen Achilles tendon turning every step into agony. "I'm smart enough to tune out all the experts," he says. "See, Mike's gotta deal with them all." His brother leans against the bus, cell phone to his ear.

The plane ride back to Phoenix would be more forlorn if not for the presence of the wives and children. The normal suspects— Marion, Bell, Kurt Thomas, House, Tucker, and Mike "Cowboy" El- liott, the assistant trainer—play poker. Nash feels like a line from "Old Man River"—body all achin' and racked with pain—but he enter- tains his twins. He *thinks* he was fouled and he *believes* he should've gotten a time-out, but he *knows* he should not have dribbled toward the midcourt sideline, either. That's the Dead Zone. The coaches vent about the referee calls—it seems they got nothing but a solid diet of bad whistles in L.A.—but they also know that the turnover on the Diaw-to-Nash inbounds play was the result of sloppy execution, and that the defense should've done a smarter job of blanketing Bryant on the tip play.

The plane ride is short and nobody even bothers turning on his video machine to review the game. Too painful. Eight months together and this is absolutely the lowest point. A television replay streams, with no audio, across the two screens in the front of the play, at one point flashing a stark graphic: Of the 160 teams that have been behind 3-1 in a playoff series, only seven have come back to win the series.

Back home, before D'Antoni turns in, he fields two phone calls. The first is from Duke coach Mike Krzyzewski, under whom D'Antoni will be an assistant this summer on the United States Olympic team. They had gotten together late in the season and hit it off.

"I'll see you soon," Krzyzewski said. Jerry Colangelo, the executive director of USA Basketball, has scheduled meetings for the Olympic coaches in Phoenix beginning on May 7, the following Saturday, also the date of a Game 7 should there be one.

"I just hope we're still playing," says D'Antoni.

Then Sarver calls with a simple message. "Kiss your wife, forget about the game, and get some sleep." D'Antoni accomplishes the first, fails miserably on the last two.

CHAPTER SEVEN

[The Second Season]

Phoenix, May 1 . . . .
LAKERS LEAD SERIES 3–1

"We're gonna have to come back here, play as hard as hell, beat their ass, and then watch the pressure go back on them. This ain't even close to being over."

Nash is the first one in the practice gym, which is not unusual. I ask him if he watched a replay of the game.

"I never do," he says. "I just went home and beat myself up. I got to sleep okay, but I woke up at 4 and couldn't get back. I got up and played with my daughters."

"Now that it's past, what bothered you the most about the jump-ball play?" I ask.

"That they didn't call the time-out," he says. "They could've called a foul. But, the time-out, I mean, Boris was screaming it. I was saying it, too, but I was concentrating on the dribble. But the refs had to have heard Boris."

Bell, meanwhile, has come down and is shooting with Weber at another basket. He is fixated on Bryant.

"What gets me is that, all of a sudden, everybody loves him again," says Bell. "And he is just not a great guy."

The remarks resonate. When Bryant scored eighty-one points against the Toronto Raptors in January, I wrote a story about it and subsequently received a couple dozen e-mails and letters criticizing me for celebrating him. They referred to Bryant's notorious rape case in Colorado (the charges were dropped), his arrogant on-court manner, or both. I didn't make any value judgments about Bryant in the story; I was writing about an athlete who had done something transcendent, which is part of my job. But when an athlete earns headlines for his exploits, there is the perception that he is being canonized as a human being. And that perception sticks in the craw of those who don't like the athlete in question.

The 3–1 deficit notwithstanding, Bell feels good about the defensive work he has done on Bryant. The Game 4 buzzer beater wasn't Bell's fault, and Bell has held Bryant in check to a greater degree than the Suns could've hoped for.

"I'm not sure I can play him any better," Bell says.

"Yes, you can," says Weber. "You're gonna play him even better in Game 5." Weber, Mr. Positive Thinker, says it with emphasis. And Bell smiles.

"Good, Phil," says Bell, "I'm glad to hear you say that. I'm gonna keep that in my mind."

The challenge for everyone, players and coaches, is to forget the horror of yesterday's game, the reality of the 3–1 deficit and the seeming mountain of calls that have gone against them and figure out what has to be done to get back in the series. The Suns just haven't played well against a team they consider to be inferior. Nash's dribble toward the corner of midcourt was un-Nash-like—he should've kept it in the middle of the floor. Iavaroni wonders, half-kiddingly, if the Suns shouldn't have tried to beat the Lakers in that late regular-season game, and maybe taken it easy in a game six days earlier against the Sacramento Kings, so that the Lakers and Kings would've flip-flopped positions. "Well, right now," says Gentry, "the Kings would be beating the dogshit out of us worse."

The feeling of malaise comes also from a general distaste for the Lakers. During a morning trip to Starbucks, at least a dozen people approached D'Antoni and told him they appreciated how the Suns had reacted to the unfortunate chain of events in Games 3 and 4. "They saw it," says D'Antoni. "Kobe's lifting up his jersey and showing his chest and doing all that stuff, and Steve is just saying, 'Well, we blew it.' At least, we're taking the high road anyway."

As the Suns see it, the Lakers trek along the low road. Bryant is arrogant. Brown is just a big body with nothing behind it. Smush Parker was a Sun for a couple of weeks last season, and no one rued his departure. Lamar Odom is just too damn big and long. Luke Walton seems like a nice guy, and his father, Bill, is a humorous announcer, but he laid out Thomas in Game 3 and triggered a miserable chain of L.A. events that ended with the nightmarish jump-ball call and the Kobe jumper. Sasha Vujacic (pronounced VU-ja-seech) is an all-universe whiner with an unpronounceable surname. Over the last week Dan D'Antoni has variously tortured it as "Vooasick," "Voojacheech," and, finally "Vooacheck." "Apparently," says Mike, "Danny thinks he's John Havlicek's younger brother." It is comparable to Dan's fused pronunciations of the surnames of Cleveland center Zydrunas Ilgauskas and Philadelphia forward Andrew Iguodala as "Inkadacus," "Ingadalis" or "Iladala." Whenever he becomes tongue-tied on a nickname, Weber says, "First day with a new mouth, Danny?"

Plus, Phil Jackson sits on a throne.

Plus, who the hell likes purple and gold?

Plus, the Lakers are kicking their ass.

There is concern among the coaches about Tim Thomas, who, after his terrific Game 1 performance, has not been much of a factor. Thomas is what is known around the league as "a ball stopper," a player who, having received a pass, holds it or dribbles it, looking for his own shot and killing a lot of clock in the process. If Thomas's shot is on, or if he can break down or successfully post up his defender, as he was able to do in Game 1, he's a valuable asset; if not, he suffocates the offense. Ball stoppers are less of a problem in standard NBA at-

89

tacks that call for isolation plays, but they are disastrous to a ball-moving team such as the Suns.

When the Suns contacted Thomas, one of those ultra-talented players who in eight previous NBA seasons had never come close to fulfilling his golden promise, he was sitting back in his home in suburban Philadelphia. Thomas had been traded from the New York Knicks to the Chicago Bulls in the preseason, but, when he arrived in Chicago, he and coach Scott Skiles were at immediate loggerheads. Skiles is one of those no-nonsense run-the-stairs-for-me type of guys; Thomas is one of those I'd-rather-take-the-elevator-and-maybe-stop-and-get-a-frappucino-along-the-way type of guys. So Skiles, in a move that was strange even by the standards of disciplinarian coaches, told him to pack up, go home and take his $13.5 million salary with him. Thomas spent the winter working out at Villanova and said he enjoyed being with his family for all the major winter holidays. Honest, that's what he said.

When Thomas came out of Patterson Catholic High School in New Jersey in 1996, he and a kid from Lower Merion, name of Kobe Bryant, were the top scholastic players in the country. Bryant opted for the NBA. Thomas, recruited by virtually every school in the country, enrolled at Villanova, which had added the carrot of hiring his uncle as an assistant coach. Thomas stayed on the Main Line for just one year—that was pretty much the understanding going in—after which the New Jersey Nets made him the seventh pick in the 1997 draft. It is astonishing how top universities make such deals and no one calls them on it. And with the NBA having raised the draft-eligibility age, there will be even more one-year college attendees. Thomas was one of the first.

Thomas said that Skiles never gave him a chance. Skiles said that Thomas was out of shape and had an attitude problem. Thomas's demeanor is not the problem for D'Antoni, but he does wonder if he has become a bad fit for the offense. "Maybe I fell into the trap of having to get bigger and stronger and loused up our offense a little bit," says D'Antoni. But the bottom line for the Suns in acquiring

Thomas was the bottom line: They are stuck for only $290,000, the prorated veteran minimum, while the Bulls are paying the rest of his comically extravagant contract. Phoenix almost couldn't afford *not* to get him, particularly with the injuries to Stoudemire and Kurt Thomas. "Pretty good rental, huh?" Iavaroni would say after Thomas had a good game. Perhaps he can be one again.

Earlier in the day, at the coaches meeting, D'Antoni had asked suddenly. "What's that porno actress's name? Del Rio? What's her first name?" It was a strange question coming from a man who had shown no previous interest in the bone-and-moan industry. Plus, he named an actress who was popular more than a decade ago.

"You gotta do better than that," says Gentry. "Go with Jenna Jameson. More recognizable. Local connection. And I guaran-damn-tee you most of our guys have seen her work."

When D'Antoni calls the team together, I say to Iavaroni: "I don't know what Mike's got planned with the porno actress, but I bet he doesn't end up using it."

"I don't know about that," says Iavaroni. "It's getting near the end of the season. You gotta use everything you got."

"All right, guys, everybody cool?" D'Antoni begins, his usual salutation. "I'm sure everybody has talked about it, rehashed it. It is what it is. Not the best thing in the world, but we gotta take something out of it. We busted their ass a couple of times and we're gonna come back and do it now. We know we can.

"We all know we're getting screwed more than Jenna Jameson . . ."—there is a titter in the gym, possibly because D'Antoni sounds so uncomfortable making the reference, possibly for other reasons—"anyway . . . I forgot what I was going to say . . . but, we're gonna have to come back here, play as hard as hell, beat their ass, and then watch the pressure go back on them. This ain't even close to being over."

I watch for signs of insincerity. Every coach has those moments when he has to out-and-out lie to his team—*Fellas, we're down forty but that's not so bad . . .* —but D'Antoni really seems to believe the Suns can come back.

"You know, you guys have gained a lot in this. The way you've handled it without going off. Public opinion is on your side. I've already had people come up to me and say how well you've handled it. The media is all over it, so let them do the talking for you. We're just going to play basketball."

Then D'Antoni moves to his and Bell's favorite subject.

"They're talking about Kobe and how great it is that he's playing with the team. Well, isn't that what you're supposed to do? Now he's the savior because he's playing that way? He's no god. He does what he's supposed to be doing, which is what we learned in kindergarten. Share the ball and play. And that's what we do better than they do. That's what we're going to do tomorrow night and get back in this thing. Everybody cool?"

The coaches usually immediately disperse after practice—they've already been together for five hours by that time—but they find themselves together in the locker-room office where D'Antoni mentions his concern about Nash's playing time. The book on Nash—and a major reason Dallas Mavericks owner Mark Cuban let him get away to Phoenix—is that he plays so hard he wears down late in the season. "If I keep him in, he gets tired," says D'Antoni, "but if I take him out, he gets stiff. He really felt it on Sunday."

"I think you have to play him almost the whole second half," says Gentry. "But you rest him like a minute or forty seconds before the time-out [the designated TV time-out] and that gives you like three minutes of rest for him."

"I hate to play without Steve at this stage of the season, but he needs some rest," says D'Antoni, thinking aloud. "I mean, I love Eddie House, and I'd like to get him in there and in the process rest Steve. But Eddie just can't get his shot off against these guys."

"I agree with you," says Gentry. "But, man, back when Eddie was shooting, we had something, didn't we?"

FULL TIME-OUT

December 15, 2005
BATON ROUGE, LA

Of Shooting Games, Tickets, and the Raiders: Eddie's in the House

The Suns' postpractice shooting games feature a revolving cast of characters, but Eddie House, "Edward Shooter Hands" as Raja Bell has taken to calling him, is almost always one of them. He usually wins. One day I asked Bell if he had ever taken any of the House money.

"Don't go there," he said in mock anger. "Get out of my face with those Eddie questions."

House has a stockpile of shots, many of which he accompanies with his own commentary.

"There's Magic Johnson across the lane, the little baby hook ... GOOD!" House says, as he replicates Magic Johnson's junior skyhook that beat the Boston Celtics in Boston Garden in Game 4 of the 1987 NBA Finals. House then trots to the sideline, where he collects imaginary high-fives from teammates.

He also has "my three-sixty," in which he twirls completely around and releases a jump shot, and another turnaround in which he takes one dribble, spins, and puts up a left-handed hook. The argument today is whether Bell is allowed to take two dribbles before shooting.

"The important thing," argues Bell, "is the shot itself, not the dribble shit."

"That ain't right," says House. "It's a whole thing I got going, and you're trying to variate my shit." To make his point, House appeals to bystanders. He grabs a ball and performs his shot, finishing it up with a loud "Ah-Ha" as he makes the move.

"What, I gotta say the 'Ah-Ha,' too?" asks Bell.

"No," says House, shaking his head, "that's the crowd respond-ing to my shit. Ah! Ha!"

December 16
BATON ROUGE, LA

A few players are sorting tickets for tonight's game against the New Orleans Hornets (who are playing several home games in Baton Rouge due to damage from Hurricane Katrina) as House looks on. I ask him if he buys many tickets for family and friends.

"Not too much anymore," says House, "because you know what happens? You buy them and leave them at the window and then the game starts and they don't show up and you're checking the stands and losing your concentration." House ponders this. "I mean, you can look for your parents in the crowd and shit," he continues, "but you can't be looking for specific motherfuckers."

"Specific motherfuckers" becomes the phrase of the week.

The pregame chatter is monopolized by talk of the NFL, which is moving into playoff season. It started when Nash says, "I don't think Terry Bradshaw is among the top twenty quarterbacks in history." Nash doesn't really care much about the subject, but there are two certified Steeler crazies in the locker room—Ohio native Jimmy Jackson and athletic trainer Aaron Nelson—and Nash knows he can get a rise out of them. Of course, Eddie House, who was born and raised in Richmond, California, hard by Oakland, wants to talk about his team, the Raiders.

"What about the Snake, Kenny Stabler?" says House. "You gotta have him high in that top twenty. Partied all night, showed up Sunday, got the job done. You got to get motherfuckin' points for that."

"We were talking about Bradshaw," says Nelson. "We weren't talking about the Raiders."

"Well, I'm talking about the Raiders," says House.

"All I know," says Jimmy Jackson, who is getting treatment from Mike Elliott, "is that the Steelers got the better franchise overall."

"First of all," says House, "why are you getting into the conversation when you're over there all isolated and shit with your headphones on?"

"I been listening the whole time," says Jackson, "just waiting to jump in and rebuttal your ass."

"Bottom line," says House, "our winning percentage is better than your winning percentage. And I'll put a thou-wow on that shit."

"Thou-wow" becomes the second phrase of the week. And he's correct about Oakland having a better all-time winning percentage.

December 28
WASHINGTON, DC

At shootaround, Alvin Gentry swishes a half-court shot, rather his specialty, to defeat House in a shooting game. Gentry runs forward, falls to his knees and says, "In the words of Brandi Chastain . . ." then strips off his shirt.

House looks over and says, "Yeah? You got titties like her, too, Alvin."

Hours later, before the game against the Wizards, the talk turns, inevitably, to the NFL again. Now, House is talking about the combine at which teams test the athleticism of college stars.

"They make a big deal about running a four-point-four," says House, talking about forty-yard dash times, "and I know I could run a four-four. You watch me tonight going to the corner. It'll be four-four shit."

"I could run that, too," says Amare' Stoudemire, who is along on the road trip though he is still out with the knee injury.

"How about nobody in this room even runs a four-*five*," says Nash. There is respectful silence for a moment—Nash doesn't often join in group bull sessions and he is presumed to have a more logical mind than anyone else.

"You telling me I can't run faster than a defensive tackle?" House says finally.

"You know a defensive tackle who can do a four-four?" asks Nash.

"There's a couple of them," says House.

"Maybe some freaks," answers Nash. "And if they can, then they're faster than you."

"How about Shawn?" chimes in D'Antoni. "Could he do a four-four?"

(An hour later, with the Suns losing to the Wizards at halftime and walking the ball up, D'Antoni derisively brings up the conversation. "Before the game we're talking about times in the forty? Shit, you have to clock us with a calendar.")

"Shawn's the one guy who could worry me," says Nash. "And L.B." (Barbosa, suffering from a sprained left knee, is not on the trip.)

But House isn't finished. "I'm telling you, I'm feeling four-four shit. You're gonna see it tonight."

That night, he misses six of his seven shots in the Suns' 104–99 victory. None of his forays down the court look very four-fourish.

December 30
CHARLOTTE, NC

House's lowest moment in the NBA came when Charlotte Bobcats coach Bernie Bickerstaff called him into his office in December 2004 and basically told him, "We don't think you're an NBA player." The Bobcats were picking up Kareem Rush, and House was told he'd be sitting behind him. Way behind him. So, House asked to be waived.

On this night in Charlotte, House is unusually serious before the game though he professes to have no special thoughts of vengeance. He scores twenty-six points, including twelve in a decisive five-minute span, as the Suns win 110–100. After one field goal, House runs back on defense, pounding his chest, glancing ever so subtly at Bickerstaff on the Charlotte bench.

After the game, Bickerstaff is asked about House. "He can make shots," says Bickerstaff, "and he sure has a strong chest."

January 2, 2006
NEW YORK, NY

House has so much shtick and seemingly so much self-confidence that it's hard to believe how many times he has been cut. There are hundreds of players like him in the NBA, high school and college stars (he still shares with UCLA's Kareem Abdul-Jabbar, then Lew Alcindor, the Pac-10 record for points scored in a single game when he got sixty-one for Arizona State against Cal in 2000) who scratch around, make a roster and live the life, but who exist in a perpetual state of anxiety. Since House was drafted in 2000, he has been unwanted by not only the Bobcats but also the Heat, L.A. Clippers, Milwaukee Bucks, and Sacramento Kings. And though he's been, to this point, everything the Suns could've wanted, he has no assurance that he will be back next season, even though his guaranteed salary of $932,000 is low.

"I thought I was sticking out in Sacramento," House says before the game. "It's tough when somebody tells you they don't want you."

He pulls out a bible and reads a passage.

"What is it?" I ask him.

"Jeremiah 29:11," he answers.

"What's it say?" I ask.

"Look it up," he says. "Maybe you'll learn something."

Later I do: *"For I know the plans I have for you," declares the Lord, "plans to prosper you and not to harm you, plans to give you hope and a future."*

CHAPTER EIGHT

[The Second Season]

Phoenix, May 2 . . . .
LAKERS LEAD SERIES 3-1

"Go be a bitch then. I'll forgive you in the morning."

When I walk into the morning coaches meeting, everybody's first words are: Did you see the paper?

Someone had e-mailed a photo of the controversial Game 4 jump-ball call to the *Arizona Republic*. It was placed on page two of the sports section. Never mind whether a foul should've been called or a time-out granted—it shows Luke Walton's foot squarely on, and in fact well over, the out-of-bounds line. Walton was the one who tied up Nash, which he could not have legally done from a position out of bounds. The photo also shows referees Bennett Salvatore and Kenny Mauer looking squarely at the play. It's impossible to conclude whether or not they can see Walton's foot, of course, but they are in perfect position to have seen it.

By morning's end, someone in Suns Nation has obtained a wider-angle version of the photo, added his or her own captions, and sent it into cyberspace. Diaw is shown running toward Nash, his mouth open, yelling.

NOT CALLING TIME-OUT reads the caption. The one above Nash reads PROFOUND SENSE OF DÉJÀ VU. The caption next to referee Salvatore reads FEELS NOTHING BECAUSE HE OBVIOUSLY SOLD HIS SOUL TO THE DEVIL (STERN). Actually, the funniest captions on the photo are next to actor David Arquette, a courtside Laker fan (STILL AMAZED HE GOT COURTNEY COX TO MARRY HIM) and a background Laker Girl (HOPING THE LAKERS SCORE A TOUCHDOWN).

Another story this morning is about the $10,000 fine that had been assessed Denver Nuggets forward Reggie Evans for grabbing the testicles of Los Angeles Clipper center Chris Kaman from behind (or, as Eddie House puts it, "right up through his ass") during a scramble for a rebound. "That's the NBA," says Gentry. "You get fined ten grand for grabbing a guy's balls and ten grand for wearing your shorts too long."

From time to time the coaches go out of their way to compliment a job done by a particular referee. Iavaroni is most likely to do it, and, occasionally, he will even take the side of an official when the coaches are reviewing a call they thought was particularly heinous. (That takes guts.) During an agonizing 139–137 triple overtime loss in Denver on January 10, Iavaroni leapt off the bench to protest a blocking call on Nash that he thought should've been a charge on the Nuggets. Joe Forte, a veteran ref, came over to the bench and said to him, "First of all, you split your pants. Second, you gotta calm down." It was true—Iavaroni was trying to get by with a pair of suit pants that had a small rip in the crotch. "I just respected the calm way Joe handled it," said Iavaroni.

But most of the time the Suns feel as if they get screwed by the zebras more than their opponents do. And every other team feels the same way. The state of refereeing is always a hot topic during the playoffs. Jermaine O'Neal of the Indiana Pacers and Shaquille O'Neal of the Miami Heat have already been fined for blasting refs. Commissioner David Stern is asked about the officiating during an impromptu news conference at the Pacers-Nets series. Stern estimates that officials make the wrong call about five percent of the time. "Right now," says David Griffin, "we're getting ninety-five percent of the five percent."

. . .

It's four hours before tip-off, and D'Antoni is a mess. "I tell you, I haven't been right since I found out Raja got hit with an extra fla-grant," he says. "That was three days ago. I know I should get it out of my head, but I can't." He fills these nervous pregame hours tinkering with matchups and listening to his iTunes, in particular a song by the artist Pink called "Dear Mr. President," an excoriating indictment of the Bush administration.

Political discussions come up with some regularity among the coaches. D'Antoni, Iavaroni, and Gentry are fervently anti–Bush. Un-der pressure, Phil Weber once admitted that he voted for Bush, and D'Antoni has never let him forget it. Dan D'Antoni tends more to-ward a form of libertarianism. Their political views parallel the broth-ers' feelings about religion. Mike and wife, Laurel, attend church together when it's possible but adhere to a liberal view of Christianity in which the church gets involved in social causes. Dan believes that all organized religions are, at root, hypocritical, in line with his politi-cal conviction that "both the Republicans and Democrats will steal you blind." The elder D'Antoni even voted for Perot back in 1992. "Danny was so eager not to get a Democrat or Republican," says Mike, "that he voted for a nut."

In the training room, meanwhile, Nash has ordered assistant trainer Mike Elliott and assistant equipment manager Jay Gaspar into the ice bath as a show of faith. Elliott and Gaspar lower themselves in, looking miserable. "Suns in seven," says Aaron Nelson, working on Nash's back.

Word comes down a couple hours before the game that Kwame Brown is being investigated for a sexual assault that allegedly hap-pened after Game 3 in Los Angeles. Reporters who meet the Laker bus for comment are greeted only by stony silence. Brown has already released a statement denying culpability. When word reaches the Suns' locker room about the story, D'Antoni asks, "Was the assault on Boris Diaw?"

The Suns come out to wild applause and the sight of the Gorilla, their inventive mascot, holding a sign that reads MISSION POSSIBLE. They seem energized and loose, beneficiaries of that magical potion known as home-court advantage. Teams in every sport do better at home, but the advantage is more pronounced in basketball; during the regular season, home teams had won about sixty percent of the time.

There are the predictable reasons. The environs are more familiar. A player slept in his own bed, ate his favorite food, drove to the arena in his favorite car, parked in his favorite spot, got good-luck messages from his favorite people around the arena. The locker room feels familiar, the pregame coffee and energy drinks are familiar, the fruit plate is familiar. This is his kingdom and, once again, he is king.

Once on the court, he gets a lift from the fans, the dance team, the banners, the messages on the video board. More than any sport, basketball (at any level) is subject to the vicissitudes of momentum, emotional ebb and flow. The fans are a factor. They are closer to the action, more organic to the flow of play. The roar in a football stadium might be literally louder than in a basketball arena, but it sure as hell doesn't *sound* louder to the players. Sound is distilled by the vastness of the stadium; it *reverberates* in a basketball arena.

Then, too, though referees and the league office would deny it, home teams generally get more favorable calls than visiting teams. How could they not? Referees are human. Lamar Odom ducks a shoulder and knocks Marion to the floor in Los Angeles. Foul on Marion. The same play in Phoenix? Offensive foul or a no-call. A few veteran referees—Steve Javie and Joey Crawford being the two most notable—are known for giving visiting teams a good whistle, sometimes all but daring the home fans to get on them. But, overall, a home team gets the majority of close ones. Put it all together, and it's home-court advantage.

Bell and Bryant walk onto the court without so much as a glance at each other. All around them is hand-slapping and good-lucking (though it does seem more subdued than usual), but their subplot of hand-to-hand combat was long ago established. *I hate you, you hate me, let's not pretend we don't hate each other.* It's actually refreshing.

The Suns jump out to a 7–0 lead. When they get up 15–5, D'Antoni feels comfortable enough to give Diaw a rest, but the Lakers get back in the game. The coach learns quickly that on this night he has to keep Diaw on the court. Diaw seems to be playing at warp speed, while Kwame Brown, perhaps distracted by the assault investigation, appears slow. The Suns outscore the Lakers 40–20 with Diaw on the court in the first half but get outscored 27–16 when he's not. Diaw converts the Suns' final eleven points of the second quarter to give them a 56–47 lead at halftime.

One of his baskets in that stretch is a resounding dunk from the wing on a fast break. Whenever Diaw finishes with a flush, it's worth at least a basket-and-a-half to the Suns. Stoudemire's injury eliminated not only twenty-six points a game but also most of the shock-and-awe component of the Phoenix attack. For an offensive-minded team, the Stoudemire-less Suns get precious few *SportsCenter* moments. Marion's Matrix moves are electrifying but there haven't been enough of them. Watching Nash weave his way through a minefield of defenders and deliver an eyes-in-the-back-of-his-head pass to a cutter is stuff for the basketball purist; crowds prefer the Stoudemire Cirque du Soleil aerials, and they can be more of a mood lifter and game changer for the team.

Diaw is a reluctant dunker, and, further, often passes out to a jump shooter when he's in position to dunk, perhaps the first center in the history of the game to even think about doing that. That pass-first mentality is a big part of what makes him unique, but there are times that the Suns wish he would just rip down the rim.

The lead reaches 73–56 midway through the third period, as a couple of Lakers glance over at Jackson to see if he wants a time-out. The be-throned coach gazes stoically into space. *Work it out yourselves, fellas.* The lead reaches 84–60 late in the third. The Suns can't let this one get away, can they? Of course they can. The Suns have shown the capacity to blow leads all season, which frustrates their fans but is understandable at some level. Since they shoot the ball quickly, there are more possessions per game for both teams. During the season Phoenix gave up a league-leading 87.09 field goal attempts per game, almost five more than second-place Denver, which also plays up-tempo. One of the keys to the Suns' success was that their defensive field goal percentage, 45.4, wasn't bad (and would've been much better had Kurt Thomas not gotten injured). Giving up a lot of shots *and* allowing the other team to make them is a prescription for disaster.

Even so, the greater the number of possessions, the more chances for the opponent to start making baskets and rallying, and, conversely, for the Suns to start missing and leaking oil. Which is exactly what happens. L.A. converts back-to-back three-point shots to close the third, then scores on five consecutive possessions to open the fourth. The crowd is getting nervous. From his courtside seat, Robert Sarver motions for the scoreboard operator to replay on the big screen any close calls that go against the Suns.

The game is getting chippy. Bell and Bryant had already drawn double technicals in the first half for jostling each other off the ball, and now they are fighting for every inch on every possession, an individual ground skirmish framed within the larger battle. The Suns have contended all series long that Bryant is a master cheap-shot artist, albeit a slick one. When he pump-fakes or shoots, he frequently manages to land an elbow on or about Bell's face. The contact takes place lower, too. Bryant comes down and rams his hip against Bell's hips. Bell pushes back, sticks his foot inside Bryant's base, tripping him up. *I hate you, you hate me, let's not pretend we don't hate each other.* Focusing on the two of them would've been a great opportunity for an isolated camera—the game within the game. When Bell complains to a referee near the Laker bench that Bryant was not whistled for an elbow, he hears a comment from Phil Jackson that includes the words "deserve it." Bell has to restrain himself from going at Jackson.

With 7:33 left in the game, the Suns fighting to sustain a double-digit advantage, and Bryant holding the ball near the free-throw line, Bell suddenly puts his left arm around Bryant's neck and horse-collars him toward the floor. As Bryant begins his descent, Bell gives a kind of what-the-fuck push with his right arm, too, as if gravity weren't sufficient to have done the job. The play is nothing short of stunning. It would've been comprehensible had they been locked up in some way, or if Bell had done it in retaliation for something overt that had happened on a previous possession. But it comes out of nowhere.

Nash, angry that his backcourt buddy has snapped, angry that the Lakers are rallying, angry about the whole combative atmosphere of this whole confounding series—this is not his kind of ball—walks over to referee Leon Wood, a former NBA player, and says, "It's you guys who caused this."

Wood is taken aback. "Not me," he says.

"You let things get out of hand," says Nash. "And this is what happens." He didn't mean Wood individually; he meant the referees collectively, including those in Games 3 and 4 in L.A.

Bell is, of course, ejected. And Bryant, as is his wont, hits a three-pointer on the next possession and the Suns lead only 93–83 with 7:17 to go. The season is in the balance, Raja Bell is in the locker room, and Kobe Bryant is on a roll.

But, then, suddenly, the Suns find the touch again. It comes, it goes; it comes, it goes. It comes. Leandro Barbosa hits a monstrous three-pointer, then Shawn Marion comes down and launches another three. Marion's unusual-looking long-distance shot, released one-handed—the Matrix goes retro—seems to reach the ceiling before it begins its slow descent. It should be accompanied by one of those air-raid whistles and a shout of "IN-COMING!" from the scoreboard. Marion gets furious when he is asked about his unorthodox shot. He feels, in that defensive way of his, that his form is being used to disrespect his game, which is not the case. It's just a source of fascination for the onlooker. There is no predicting whether a Marion three-pointer will (a) sail over the basket, as it sometimes does when he shoots it from the corner, (b) fail to reach its target, as it sometimes does from anywhere, or (c) settle blessedly into the basket, not unusual since he is a career thirty-five percent three-point shooter, a good number for someone whose marksmanship is so suspect.

This one goes in. The Suns go on to score six more points before the Lakers get a basket, and it's over.

With 3:11 left and the issue decided, Bryant complains to Wood about a call and draws a second technical and automatic ejection. Wood gets no love from either side for the call. The Lakers figure that he did it in response to Nash's complaining, and the Suns figure that he took a stand too late. Bryant smirks as he leaves the court, shaking his head, and the enmity toward the NBA's most talented player pours down upon him. KO-BE SUCKS! KO-BE SUCKS!

As time winds down on the 114–97 win, Alvin Gentry finally gives voice to something he had been holding in the entire game. "Danny," he says to Dan D'Antoni. "you got on two different shoes." Gentry had noticed it early in the game but didn't want to mention it as long as the outcome was in doubt. "I just kept praying, 'Please let us win so I can bust him, please let us win so I can bust him,'" says Gentry. He alerts the bench and Stoudemire shakes his head. "Damn, Coach Dan," he says, "you can't be wearing a lizard on one foot and a gator on the other."

The Suns are ecstatic with the win, of course, but a sense of uncertainty immediately sets in. They try to sell the idea that the pressure is back on the Lakers, but Game 6 is in Los Angeles, and Bell, already on double secret probation and maybe even on double-double secret probation, will almost certainly be suspended.

Julie Fie convinces Bell that he should go to the interview room and fall on the sword. She has a vague worry that Raja will soliloquize about Bryant's defects as a human being, but, she figures, he's a smart guy who can be a diplomat when so required.

As Bell gets dressed, Tim Thomas says, with a big smile, "Don't be a bitch to the media now."

"They tell me that's my only chance," says Raja.

"I understand," says Thomas. "Go be a bitch then. I'll forgive you in the morning."

Almost lost in the hubbub about Bell is the play of Diaw, who finishes just one assist shy of a triple-double—twenty-five points (including 11-of-11 from the free-throw line) and ten rebounds. "Boris Jordan" they call him in the locker room.

"I don't know where we'd be without that kid," says Gentry. "From where he started to where he is now? It's one of the most amazing things I've ever seen, I can tell you that."

FULL TIME-OUT

October 9, 2005
TRAINING CAMP, TUCSON

Getting to Know the Frenchman

As befitting someone with a curious mind and disposable income, Boris Diaw got the news that he had been traded to the Phoenix Suns while on safari in Africa. To put it generously, Diaw was an afterthought in the acrimonious deal that sent Joe Johnson, a mainstay starter during the 2004–05 renaissance season, to Atlanta. General manager Bryan Colangelo thought Diaw was good and assistant GM Dave Griffin thought he was *real* good, but almost no one else in the Suns' organization even knew him. "Who's the Russian?" asked Alvan Adams, a Suns' legend as a player and now the arena manager, when he heard about the trade last August.

Diaw had averaged 4.8 points, 2.6 rebounds, and 2.3 assists in Atlanta, a team that finished with a 13-69 record, worst in the league. Colangelo and Griffin insist that Diaw never got the opportunity to demonstrate his versatility in Atlanta. The coaches don't know enough about Diaw to confirm that, reserve players on cellar-dwelling teams commanding little time in scouting reports. At the very least, he has innate athletic ability. His Senegalese father, Issa Diaw, was once an outstanding high jumper. His mother, Elisabeth Riffiod, is considered one of France's all-time great women basketball players. Diaw the Younger can do a lot of things, but, sometimes in the NBA, that is a negative. A player needs a position. The Suns coaches are less wedded to that concept than most teams, but even they can't quite decide what Diaw is. Backup point guard, which is what he played (more or less) with Atlanta? Small forward? Power forward? He's six-feet-eight—can he guard some of the smaller centers?

Whatever, the coaches are sure of one thing: They desperately miss Johnson, who had been a free agent at the end of last season. Owner Robert Sarver did not see Johnson in quite the same light as the coaches. Sarver saw a fourth wheel who was not nearly as important to the Suns' future as Steve Nash, Amare' Stoudemire, or Shawn Marion, certainly not with a big-dollar deal with Stoudemire in the works. Sarver was willing to offer Johnson a six-year deal worth $75 million. That sounds generous, but in the NBA, as in the Fortune 500 world, worth is skewed and relative. The Hawks, looking to rebuild behind Johnson, offered $70 million, front-loading $19 million of it. Sarver wasn't ready to make that kind of commitment and said, "Work out a trade."

Even the coaches weren't absolutely sure Johnson was worth that money. But they knew they had lost a six-foot-seven-inch warrior who guards multiple positions, runs tirelessly (Johnson is among the perennial leaders in minutes played), and creates his own shot in the half-court. "One thing we can't replace," says Phil Weber, "is Joe's ability to get into the lane and take over parts of the game."

Nash, Marion, and Stoudemire had been penciled in as starters from the beginning of camp, of course, with Kurt Thomas (center) and Raja Bell (shooting guard) probably joining them. Behind them were a lot of question marks, of which Diaw was one. Personnel matters had gotten even more complicated, however, when it became known that Stoudemire would probably require knee surgery.

Now the rotation gets murky, the inevitable ripple effect caused by an injury to a prime player. Someone has to replace Stoudemire in the starting lineup, and that someone would've been a sixth or seventh man, so now that someone has to take the new starter's minutes, and someone has to take the other someone's minutes, and next thing you know a couple of guys are playing more minutes than they should. Extended minutes reveal deficiencies.

"If we can get twenty-four minutes with Shawn at four, and

twenty-four with Kurt Thomas or Brian Grant, we'll be fine," says D'Antoni. "That gives me time to play James Jones, Eddie House, Boris Diaw, or whoever. But can we play eleven guys? Ten guys? Hell, nine guys?" There are many responsibilities that separate a head coach from his assistants, but none starker than the burden of playing time. Assistants suggest substitution patterns and offer opinions on which players have earned extra minutes. But the head coach pulls the trigger, and D'Antoni has begun worrying about playing time from the first moment of camp.

"A lot of it is on Brian Grant, and whether he can keep up," says Dan D'Antoni. Grant is a cagey thirty-three-year-old veteran who signed a free agent contract with the Suns in the off-season. Even with bad knees, Grant is a bargain for the Suns, who are paying him $1.7 million, although he's into the Lakers for $14.5 million (and $15.6 million the following year), the result of a huge deal he originally signed with the Portland Trail Blazers.

"Pat Burke is going to be the eleventh man," says D'Antoni. "Nothing against him, but somebody's gotta be. Now, between Boris Diaw, Eddie House, L.B., and Brian Grant, one of those four have to be number ten."

"In my mind it's going to be B.G.," says Dan. "I watched that clear-out and they were blowing by him. He had no chance. And it wasn't because he was tired. He's in good shape."

"Brian Grant is competing against Eddie and L.B. for minutes," says D'Antoni, "even though he's not their position."

"He's competing against style," says Dan.

"Well, what everyone is playing against is how good Boris Diaw plays in our system," says D'Antoni. "Can he be a legit backup power forward?"

"What I worry about, with Boris, is his attitude," says Alvin Gentry. "He just doesn't seem to want to learn."

"Boris is in your head, Coach," says Iavaroni, smiling.

"Damn right he is," answers Gentry.

"Look, it's tough in two-a-days," says Iavaroni. "Let's get back to Phoenix and work with him."

"You try to get Boris to do anything in practice he doesn't want to do, and it's tough," says Dan.

"Put it this way," says Weber, "you have to have *discussions* with Boris." Weber has already started working with Diaw on his jump shot. Though Diaw is never likely to become a three-point shooter, the Suns would like to see him become a perimeter threat. Diaw seems to have his own ideas on shooting drills, and most everything else. Which is perhaps to be expected from someone whose full name is Boris Babacar Diaw-Riffiod. It sounds like he should have "Marquis" in front of his name. But if anyone can break him down, it's Weber, a tireless clinician.

"I know I shouldn't say anything to Boris," says Gentry. "I mean, he won a whole thirteen games last year in Atlanta. What did we win, sixty-two?"

For all of that, there is something likable about Diaw. There is the suggestion of arrogance about him—"I do not date American women," he says, "I *have* them"—but also the suggestion of class and refinement. And he is unfailingly upbeat with a word of greeting for everyone. "How are you doo-EENG?" Diaw says to whomever he sees, a refreshing change from the American *howyadoin*. And Diaw's sing-songy "thank you"—which sounds like "sank youuuu!"—is already being replicated around the locker room. Eddie House has been caught practicing it.

But, all in all, Diaw looks like a problem for D'Antoni on whom the distribution of minutes, as well as the burden of owner and fan expectation after sixty-two wins in the previous season, falls. And he will be trying to accomplish all that without Stoudemire (for at least four months), three-point threat Quentin Richardson (who went to the Knicks so the Suns could add Kurt Thomas for interior strength), and Joe Johnson. And *with* a joyfully cantankerous, or cantankerously joyful question mark from France named Boris Diaw. "Boris is probably just good enough to get us all fired," concludes D'Antoni.

At this early checkpoint, then, Boris Diaw is one step above a "whoever," a certified attitude problem, a possible backup power forward, a possible tenth man, and a possible coach killer. Good thing the front office likes him.

CHAPTER NINE

[The Second Season]

May 3 . . . .
LAKERS LEAD SERIES 3–2

"Do I know this guy? I don't know this guy. I might've said one word to this guy. I don't know this kid."

Jerry Colangelo brought the Suns into the NBA in 1968. He coached them, general-managed them, scouted for them, and owned them, and, two years after selling the team to Robert Sarver, is still chairman and CEO. Beyond that, Colangelo is rather the Godfather of the NBA, and not just because he is a tough Italian. Over the years, he is the one who makes the secret deals and knows where all the bodies are buried, strictly in the figurative sense. Over the last two decades, as David Stern has expanded his power to become the commissioner of commissioners, Colangelo is the only team executive who has consistently had Stern's ear.

Colangelo's place in the Suns' hierarchy is now tenuous. His son, Bryan, left his job as general manager after a midseason dispute with Sarver, and now Sarver and Colangelo circle each other warily, like two panthers angling for space in the same small cage. But Jerry is still the top figure on the franchise flow chart (his contract as chairman/ CEO runs until June of 2007), and, when Jerry speaks, Suns Nation listens. And it was decided immediately after Game 5 that Jerry should make the call to Stu Jackson to plead the case for Raja Bell.

"Here's how I laid it out," Colangelo tells D'Antoni. "I told him

112

he kind of owes us one. Three miscues [no foul call, no time-out call, Walton out-of-bounds] cost us Game 4. 'Do you think that was important, Stu? Losing a game we should've won and going down 3–1?' Then there was the technical not called on Kwame Brown when he stood over our guy and glared at him. The stray elbows. The Kobe theatrics with pulling the jersey over his head when a technical wasn't called either." As a last resort, Colangelo also suggested to Jackson: "If you have to suspend Bell, why not make it for two games at the beginning of next season?"

Even with Colangelo at bat, everyone in the Suns' organization knows this: There is positively, absolutely no chance that Raja Bell—a marked man even before the playoffs started—won't be suspended. "Johnnie Cochran couldn't get him off," concludes Alvin Gentry at the morning coaches meeting.

"Johnnie's dead," says Phil Weber.

"So's Raja," says Gentry.

Though no one will concede the point, Colangelo's preemptive lobbying is as much about discouraging Jackson from suspending Bell for *two* games, a distinct possibility. The coaches study the photo of the clotheslining that appears on page one of the *Arizona Republic*. There is no abundance of love for Kobe Bryant within the Suns' franchise, but everyone admits there are legitimate grounds for indictment. "I tell you guys, Kobe could have gotten really hurt there," says Gentry. "The league can't allow that."

At 9 a.m., athletic trainer Aaron Nelson calls up to the coaches room. "NBA security just asked for Raja's number," reports Nelson. The hammer will be coming down soon.

"What I worry about is from this one angle it just looks like Raja is rearing back and throwing the forearm, like a punch," says Dave Griffin.

"Maybe because he kind of was?" I add helpfully.

"And then they put it on page one for all the world to see," says Gentry.

I feel obligated to speak up for my newspaper brethren. "Any newspaper that didn't put that photo on page one wouldn't be doing its job."

"Oh, I'm not saying that," says Gentry. "I would've put it on page one, too, if I was the editor."

The task now is to strategize with the assumption that Leandro Barbosa will be starting in place of Bell. Having Barbosa in the starting lineup makes the Suns even more, well, Suns-like. Barbosa is perhaps the fastest player in the league with the ball, Philadelphia's Allen Iverson and Dallas's Devin Harris being his only competitors. Despite an orthodox, almost two-handed release on his jump shot, he is an excellent three-point shooter, having finished the season with a .444 percentage on three-point shots, best on the team and third best in the league. He has a six-foot-ten-inch wingspan that enables him to get off shots in heavy traffic. In short, he is a better offensive player than Bell.

But L.B. is not nearly as good a defender. Bell has been a rock defensively, fundamentally sound, and, above all, tough. The Suns use part of their accrued fine money to pay fifty bucks for every charging foul drawn, and Bell had picked up $3,650 during the season for drawing seventy-three, best in the league. There's a saying around the league that "the more money you make, the less you take a charge," but that doesn't apply to Bell. After finally getting a good contract—the Suns gave him $23.8 million over five years, a free-agent deal that at least one pundit termed the worst of the summer—Bell threw his body around like a Hollywood stuntman. Oddly, he became known as both a tough guy and a flopper, i.e., a player who exaggerates contact and falls backward or down with the exuberance of a stage actor. As to the latter, Bell prefers to say that he is merely "emphasizing a call that should be made."

Barbosa, slightly built at six-foot-three and 188 pounds, gets pushed around. He has much to learn about positioning and plays too much with his hands, reaching out and grabbing, a personal foul waiting to happen. Barbosa is not a bad defender by any means—he is quick, willing, and tough-minded—but in Game 6, another elimination challenge, he will be asked to check the game's best player.

There is really no alternative plan, though. Marion could guard Bryant, but that would force Diaw into guarding Marion's man, Lamar Odom, and the Suns don't like that matchup. The biggest worry for the coaches is that Barbosa will be unable to gold Bryant, i.e., front him to discourage an entry pass, a stratagem that Bell has been using effectively. The Suns know that their double-teams on Bryant have to be more forceful than they were with Bell on the court.

"L.B.'s got to know when he can deny him and when he can't," says Dan D'Antoni, "but most of all he has to realize that it's not the end of the world when he does score."

There is no doubt that Barbosa will take the challenge, for no one works more diligently at improving. That fact, his boyish innocence, his occasional torturing of the English language ("Nobody was believing myself at that time" is his way of saying that he surprised a lot of people around the NBA), his sincere love for his family back in Brazil, and about a dozen other things make Barbosa the most beloved player on the team.

In one of the golden school-trip moments, I can still see Barbosa in the back of the bus as it headed for the airport in Toronto on the morning of April 1 after a win over the Raptors the night before. A spontaneous chorus of "O Canada" broke out, and Barbosa, with a big smile on his face, waved his arms like a conductor. He wasn't singing, probably because he had no idea what the words were—he was just smiling and conducting. He had grown up a poor kid in São Paulo, Brazil, learning the game from his older brother, Arturo, a taskmaster who used to whack him with a stick when he made the wrong move during ball-handling drills. A small scar runs along the base of Barbosa's left thumb bears memory to their workouts. And there he was conducting "O Canada" in an NBA bus.

"If you don't like L.B.," says Dan D'Antoni, who has become

Barbosa's personal coach, assigned by his brother to that task early in the season, "there's something wrong with *you*."

Nash is out shooting early on the practice court when Bell, somewhat sheepishly, walks in. "There he is!" shouts Nash, as if announcing the appearance of a rock star. Bell waves and smiles, though he is a little embarrassed. By any logical reckoning, Bell's flagrant foul on Bryant was a brainless act. It occurred when the outcome was still in the balance, Bell was not retaliating to contact (indeed, Bryant was alone in the middle of the court; it was akin to a mugging), and, moreover, he was jeopardizing the entire series. Yet there is universal support for Bell within the team. The coaches love Bell not just for his competitiveness but also for his loyalty. Shortly after he signed his free-agent contract, the Suns went after another free agent, Michael Finley, and, though signing Finley would've meant less playing time for Bell, he was among those who went on Finley's "recruiting trip." (Finley eventually signed with San Antonio.)

The support for Bell is predictable on one level: He who does not stand up for a teammate in time of need is a traitor. But there is also the fact that throughout the season and in this series, the Suns are always the team that is considered soft, always the team that gets pushed around. Bell himself had noted that weeks earlier, during halftime of a game in Sacramento on April 11, one of the more memorable nights of the year. The Suns trailed the Kings by 68–51 and appeared to be mailing it in at every position. Including coach. D'Antoni had been down on himself for failing to ignite his team, which, having all but mathematically clinched second place in the Western Conference, seemed to be drifting along, content with the world, failing to build playoff momentum. At the break, D'Antoni went at the team, but then Bell asked to speak, and his words, delivered calmly but forcefully, were the ones that made the difference.

"Right now they think we're their 'hos," Bell said. "And I want to tell you something: I ain't nobody's 'ho. There comes a time when we gotta go out there and change what people think of us because, right now, people think of us as pussies. I'm going to do it right now. This half."

And the Suns responded with their best concentrated play of the season. Eight of them scored at least nine points apiece. They made 71 percent of their shots. They scored seventy-two points. They weren't nobody's 'ho. They won going away, 123–110, against a home team that had won six of its previous seven games. That game helped reposition the Suns, in their own minds, as a championship contender.

I wander over to Bell and ask if he has heard from the league.

"Not yet," he says, "but I expect I will."

Then I ask, with all due care, "So, um, why did you do it?" It seems better than, *What the hell were you thinking?*

Bell shakes his head. "It's like it happened in slow motion," he says. " 'All right, Rah-Rah, don't do it. Don't . . . you're going to do it . . . you're going to do it . . . SHIT! You did it.' " Bell says he was also angered because Phil Jackson said to him, "You fuckin' deserve it," when he protested about a noncall on Bryant.

Bell admits to a history that includes more than a few scuffles on and off the court. During his sophomore year at Boston University a coach sent him to a sports psychologist to discuss anger management. Bell attended a couple of sessions but nothing much came of it. "I didn't dig it," he says. "I never thought I had an anger problem. I just thought I was trying to find out who I was, trying to figure out how I fit in. In retrospect, yeah, maybe I could've talked to somebody. It might've helped me out a little bit."

Like, say, when it was time for Bell to take his league-mandated urine test a month earlier. He just couldn't produce under pressure and became so incensed that he almost tossed away his cup and walked out, which would result in an automatic suspension. "Raja, you can't get mad at a urine test," Dave Griffin told him. Bell stuck around and finally came through in the clutch. On numerous occasions during the season, Bell would go into a minitantrum, walking off the court and talking to himself, after missing three straight jumpers in practice. The assistant throwing him the ball, usually Gentry or Weber, would calmly wait for Bell to settle himself, and the warm-up would begin anew.

Bell's temper caused him and D'Antoni—mutual admirers—to get into it after the San Antonio Spurs drubbed the Suns 117–93 in Phoenix on March 9. It was a miserable night all around. Nash was out with a badly sprained right ankle. Barbosa had shown up for the game with a painful groin injury from one of his testicles having gotten twisted in its sack—"That's some Third World shit right there," said Iavaroni—and didn't play either. Marion and Tim Thomas were both recovering from the flu. The Spurs dominated for forty-eight minutes, and Bell, like almost everyone else, played poorly. Bell had snapped at Diaw during the game. "Pass the damn ball!" he said, an unfair criticism since Diaw had played unselfishly. Later, Bell angered D'Antoni when, in the coach's mind, he had pretended not to hear a play call that he had actually heard. So D'Antoni had snapped at him during a time-out.

After the game, D'Antoni decided to extend an olive branch to Bell. "All right, I shouldn't have done that with Raja," he says. "Raja, I apologize. We cool?" Bell didn't say anything or even look up. So D'Antoni repeated it. "Raja, we cool?" Finally, Bell sullenly nodded. That was not the Yalta moment D'Antoni had been looking for, and he lectured the team for ten minutes, after which Bell still looked angry. Coach and player then conferred behind closed doors, but the matter didn't get cleared up until two nights later when, before a game against Minnesota, Bell apologized to the team for snapping at Diaw.

"Raja will go off from time to time," says D'Antoni, "but if I had twelve guys like him, I'd feel pretty good."

Bell comes by his temper naturally. Presented with the Kobe

challenge, Bell's father, Roger, an athletic administrator at the University of Miami, would've possibly done something worse than a horse collar. Roger Bell has twice been kicked out of fifty-and-over basketball tournaments for overaggressiveness, one time breaking an opponent's nose. Raja, his mother, and his sister, Tombi, who was an outstanding college player, were there to enjoy the spectacle.

"I mean, damn, fifty-and-over, you'd think you'd be able to chill by that time," says Bell. "But I understand it because my dad and I have the same temperament. We lose it, then, by the time we get back in the car, it's 'Oops, we shouldn't have done that.' Some people who don't know me think I'm a complete asshole. I understand that. I know I'm not. I'm not like that at home at all. But, when I get on that court and people try to take something from me or get over on me, I *will* fight."

Though they are different types of players, Bell's career parallels that of Eddie House. They have both battled, convinced they have the talent to make it but looking for a coach to confirm it. They have to find a way to stay on the court, a way to get an identity. With House, it's shooting. With Bell, it's pit-bull defense and midrange competence.

Bell is convinced, or he is trying to convince himself, that his team will be just fine without him in Game 6. "Either Kobe's going to be passive and it won't matter," he says, "or he'll try to take over and dominate L.B. and mess everything else up."

When D'Antoni gathers the team together, he doesn't begin with the let's-get-fired-up-and-win-it-for-Raja speech. He wants to make it seem like any other game (though clearly it is not) so he goes over matchups and the importance of being as active on defense as they were in Game 5. Almost off-handedly, he says, "We'll get word about Raja soon. Whatever happens, I don't have any doubt we'll handle it. As the games go on, the Lakers are getting a little tighter. Trust me on that. It's going to be a great atmosphere. This is fun. This is what it's about."

After practice, Bell, obviously, is the big story. The press contingent is large, and everyone wants Raja. Julie Fie is nervous about letting him speak, but, in keeping with the Suns' policy, she makes Bell available after practice, an open target. He answers a few harmless questions, and then Fie, hovering around the outside of the group, hears the words "no respect for him," "pompous," and "arrogant." She swoops in and puts her hand gently on Bell's back, just to let him know she's there. But Bell is rolling, and Fie, with more than two decades in the business, recognizes a lost cause when she sees it.

"I think a lot of people let him get away with things and he feels like he's supposed to get away with them and I don't agree with that," Bell says of Bryant. "If you're going to keep hitting me in my face and then talking like you're not doing it on purpose . . . there's a reason both of my cheeks are bruised right now and I can barely open my jaw. Every time you stick your butt out [he means when Bryant posts him up by the foul line] and try to hit me in my genitals [he really says "genitals"], you're doing it on purpose. That's something you don't do inadvertently and it was enough."

Last night, after the game, Bryant had jokingly said maybe he and Bell should take their battle into the Octagon, the venue for Ultimate Fighting. Bell sniffs when someone brings that up. "We don't need an Octagon. There's plenty of space and opportunity right out on the court, man. When I get hit in the face multiple times, you've stepped across a line with me. It's not basketball anymore."

Bell also revealed the exchange he had had with Jackson during the game. "I thought that was kind of bush league from such a good coach," says Bell.

Out in Los Angeles, Jackson confirms that he and Bell did have words, though he obviously has a different take on it. "I told him, 'You're leaning in there all the time, so you deserve it,'" says Jackson. The coach says he did not use the F-word. And Jackson also pooh-poohs the notion that the series is physical. "Fifteen years ago guys were thrown up into the seats, and it was really rough," says the coach.

"I think they're much more on edge than is necessary in this series. My guys are pussycats, and Phoenix has a bunch of pussycats, too."

Word has spread about Bell's comments, and Bryant is ready, returning to the I-am-king-and-I'm-not-sure-who-he-is theme. "Does he know me?" says Bryant. "Do I know this guy? I don't know this guy. I might've said one word to this guy. I don't know this kid. I think he overreacts to stuff. We go out there, we play and when we play during the season, we play each other. That's it. I don't know this kid. I don't need to know this kid. I don't want to. We go out there, we play the game and we leave it at that. Maybe he wasn't hugged enough as a kid. I look at him a little bit, he gets a little insecure or something."

If you're scoring at home, that's four "kids" and three "guys."

Kobe also says that Bell has "a glass jaw," and denies deliberately attacking Bell's genitals. "Whoa, I'm nowhere near doing something like that. We're out there playing basketball. He's a good defender. He's a good basketball player. Just go out there and play the game. There's no need to whine about it."

NBA Commissioner David Stern also weighs in on the Bell flagrant. He calls it "unmanly."

The one-hour flight to Los Angeles is quiet. It was decided among the players—in effect, by Bell, Nash, and Brian Grant, who are more or less the travel counselors, their wives being more or less the wives-in-chief—that significant others should not come along on the trip. It will be short and all business, and, superstitiously, no one had to bring up the fact that the Suns lost both games in L.A. when families were in tow. Jason March, the assistant video coordinator (whom Nash calls "Raef LaFrentz" because he bears a strong resemblance to that NBA player), was along on the Game 3 and 4 trip, too, and he took a lot of heat for being a jinx. So he's back in Phoenix.

At dinner, D'Antoni is asked what particular referees he doesn't want to see. He names one. "We just seem to have a personality con-flict," he says. "It's partly my fault, too. But we just don't get along." Not thirty seconds later, that ref walks by, having chosen to dine in the same restaurant. That means he will be working tomorrow night. He and the coach share polite nods. Between clenched lips, D'Antoni says: "Do I have the worst karma in the world, or what?"

CHAPTER TEN

[The Second Season]

Los Angeles, May 4 . . . .
LAKERS LEAD SERIES 3–2

"Make sure you mention Shawn. We couldn't have done it without him."

Raja Bell, who to everyone's immense relief has been suspended for only tonight's game, has decided to attend the morning shootaround. The only restriction on him in Los Angeles is that he must be out of the Staples Center two hours before tip-off.

"If you think that's the best thing to do, go for it," says Iavaroni, gently questioning whether in fact it is the best thing.

"Nobody told me not to," says Bell. "I'm not going to talk to the media, though. I did my talking yesterday."

Indeed, Bell's and Bryant's comments about each other dominate the morning sports pages in Los Angeles, as they do back in Phoenix. But the way the situation was handled by Julie Fie and John Black was absolutely correct. Some NBA teams would've kept Bell and Bryant from commenting, a ridiculous alternative. The players are grown men in the public eye, and they should get the chance to express their feelings. And what is the dire consequence if those feelings come out as antagonistic? It's not like the basketball-watching public isn't aware of the enmity the players hold toward each other.

One can only imagine what would've happened had this situation involved the clueless Portland Trail Blazers, who weeks earlier had announced a new media policy in which interviews with executives and players might be tape-recorded by the team, with a transcript or audio file of the interview posted on the Blazers' website. Also, reporters will be asked in some cases to provide a written list of questions before being granted an interview. The Blazers collect a bunch of reprobate players, blame the media when the inevitable negative stories come out, then construct policies that assure continued negative public relations. Today, that is what passes for media relations in some professional cities.

Besides, somewhere in the NBA offices in New York City, a few executives were silently conceding that a war of words is a good thing. One of the NBA's biggest problems with the consumer is the perception that the game is passionless, that teammates and opponents are bonded by a feeling of joint entitlement, and that those memorable and venomous team-against-team rivalries, such as the Lakers-Celtics and Pistons-Bulls, have gone the way of the two-handed set shot.

Bell has read Bryant's comments about him, and, even if he hadn't, everyone is quick to relay them to him. "See, to Kobe," says Bell, "this is like a movie. It isn't real life. To me, this is real. But one thing I learned is that they're going to spin everything and make Kobe look good." Bell doesn't identify who "they" might be, and his statement is a vast exaggeration anyway. The Kobe haters, and there are legions of them, will continue to hate him, and the Kobe lovers, or loyal Laker fans, will continue to love him. The new development is that Raja Bell—*I don't know this kid. I don't need to know this kid*—is now more than a blip on the NBA radar screen. He has an identity, which he has been looking for throughout his career at the fringes of NBA legitimacy.

At practice, Barbosa works with the first team, but D'Antoni does call on Bell later. "Raja," says the coach during a defensive drill, "get in here and be Kobe." Says D'Antoni: "I couldn't resist that."

• • •